From High School To Headlocks
An Unlikely Pro Wrestling Story

Eric Perez

From High School To Headlocks: An Unlikely Pro Wrestling Story

Author: Eric Perez

Year: 2023

Copyright © 2023 Eric Perez

All rights reserved.

No part of this publication may be reproduced, distributed, or transmitted in any form or by any means, including photocopying, recording, or other electronic or mechanical methods, without the prior written permission of the publisher, except in the case of brief quotations embodied in critical reviews and certain other noncommercial uses permitted by copyright law. Thank you for respecting the hard work of this author.

For permissions requests or inquiries, please contact Eric Perez at ericandrewperez@gmail.com.

ISBN: 9798856780979

Published by Eric Perez

United States

Cover design by Eric Perez

Interior layout and design by Eric Perez

Printed in United States

Copyright © 2023 Eric Perez

To Mom & Dad

Table of Contents

Introduction..1

Chapter 1
A Childhood Obsession...5

Chapter 2
Bumping with Beanie Babies:
Learning to Wrestle..43

Chapter 3
Lights, Camera, Action:
The Debut Match 65

Chapter 4
Navigating Wrestling's
'He Said, She Said Bullshit'...89

Chapter 5
Back to Square One:
Relearning in the Wrestling World............................115

Chapter 6
Wrestling's Evolution:
Choosing Ring Lights Over Prom Night 149

Chapter 7
The Unintended Legacy of
'The Dude Who Wrestles Girls'..................................169

Chapter 8
Working with the Big Leagues:
Avoiding Bubba's Fury..197

Chapter 9
Road Trip Chronicles:
How I Accidentally Became 'Joey'..................217

Chapter 10
From Sober to Supershot:
How I Drank My Way to My Gimmick..................239

Chapter 11
Tales of Wrestling Pranks and
Bathroom Shenanigans..................261

Chapter 12
Wrestling Ring Legends:
Battling Ho's and Kings!..................277

Chapter 13
Favorite Matches & Crazy Moments: From Light Tubes to Easter Eggs..................299

Chapter 14
Passing the Torch:
Shaping Wrestling's Future..................339

Chapter 15
Behind the Curtain: From the Ring to the Booker's Chair..........349

Chapter 16
From the Mat to the Heart:
Closing Reflections..................365

Special Thanks..................379

Introduction

Writing this autobiography about my wrestling journey has been a deeply introspective and humbling experience. When I first considered this endeavor I questioned whether my story was significant enough to share with the world. As I sat down to piece together this book, I must admit, it was no walk in the park. I found myself questioning whether my stories were exciting enough, whether my experiences were noteworthy, or if anyone would even care about my journey. I mean, who wants to hear about a regular guy like me stumbling through the ropes of the wrestling world?

But you know what? As I sifted through the memories I realized that sometimes, it's the ordinary tales that hold the most charm. As I reflected on the past, I realized that my journey, though not that of a mega star, is one filled with valuable lessons and genuine passion. If anything it's a guide of what NOT to do in the wrestling business.

All jokes aside, I have learned a lot with my time in the wild world of professional wrestling and I am happy to finally share it with those that are interested to learn about my journey. Throughout my 20 plus year wrestling tenure, I have encountered trials and tribulations that have shaped me in ways I could never have imagined.

From my teenage years, to my adult age, I've faced both triumphs and setbacks, joys and challenges. It's been a path that demanded dedication and perseverance, often requiring me to overcome my own doubts and insecurities. My experiences may not be those of a superstar but they are real and honest, and I believe there's value in that authenticity.

As you turn the pages of this autobiography I hope you learn something new, not just about professional wrestling, but about me from this candid and genuine journey. Mine is a tale of resilience and determination, filled with stories of laughter, pain and even love.

I hope that by sharing my experiences I can offer insights into the real-world challenges of pursuing a dream in the wrestling world, encouraging others to pursue their passions with wisdom and humility.

This book is for anyone who's had dreams, big or small, and wanted to chase them. I really hope this book gives you the inspiration to keep moving ahead, no matter how many doubts you might be dealing with.

From the bottom of my heart, I am absolutely proud to share my story. Thank you for being a part of this journey with me. From High School to Headlocks, this is a story of dreams pursued, obstacles overcome and the unyielding love for a sport that has shaped my life in ways I will forever cherish.

Sincerely,
Eric Perez
(Joey Spector)

4

Chapter 1
A Childhood Obsession

My journey into the world of professional wrestling began in an unexpected way when my family moved to San Antonio, Texas in 1996. Moving to San Antonio was like stepping into a whole new world. Leaving my friends back in Fort Worth made the transition even harder, especially since I moved during the summer when school was out, and there weren't many opportunities to meet new people.

As my 12th birthday approached that July, I couldn't help but feel a bit lonely. Celebrating without my old friends by my side made me miss Fort Worth even more. I longed for that sense of belonging I once had. Moving to San Antonio and leaving behind my childhood friends was an incredibly challenging experience for me.

I felt completely lost in this new city and couldn't help but despise my new surroundings. The longing to be back with my old friends was overwhelming, and I found myself crying every day, pouring my heart out to my parents, begging them to let me return to my old school and reunite with the familiar faces I had grown up with.

However, just when I thought things would stay that way, fate had something else in store for me. Next door, there was a lively house filled with boys around my age. Their laughter and constant togetherness piqued my curiosity, and I felt drawn to join them. So, with a mix of nerves and excitement, I mustered the courage to approach them while they were playing football outside. Wrestling wasn't even on my radar until I found myself at their house one evening. The flickering glow of the television screen introduced me to WCW Monday Nitro. Little did I know that this chance encounter would ignite a passion that would shape the course of my life.

Before my family moved to San Antonio, I had occasional glimpses of WWE and WCW while growing up, and I was vaguely aware of some of the wrestling legends like Hulk Hogan, Ric Flair, Macho Man and Sting. However, I had never truly immersed myself in the world of professional wrestling until that fateful moment when I stumbled upon WCW Monday Nitro at my next-door neighbor's house.

As the colorful characters, epic clashes and dramatic storytelling unfolded on the television screen, something within me clicked. The magic of wrestling took hold of my heart and I found myself captivated by the spectacle before me. It was as if the world of wrestling had been waiting for the perfect moment to draw me in and that night was the turning point.

From that very moment, wrestling became more than just a form of entertainment. It became a way of life, a mesmerizing world of excitement and possibilities that had me eagerly tuning in every week, hungry for the next thrilling chapter of the wrestling saga. The episodic nature of WCW Monday Nitro had me hooked, and I became a devout fan, eager to catch every electrifying moment that unfolded in that squared circle.

Three decades have passed since those early days, and yet the passion for pro wrestling continues to burn as brightly as ever within me. The tradition of tuning in to Monday night wrestling has endured and it's now a shared experience between me and my dad. The journey we embarked upon all those years ago has not only shaped my life but also forged an unbreakable bond between us.

Our shared enthusiasm for wrestling has acted as a constant thread weaving through the fabric of our relationship. Beyond the spectacle of the matches and the story lines, it's the conversations, the debates and the shared excitement that have truly brought us closer together as father and son.

Back in 1996, as the new kid in town, finding my place in a new school might have been a challenge, but wrestling proved to be the catalyst that brought me together with my newfound group of friends at Woodlake Hills Middle School. We connected over our shared love for wrestling and it wasn't long before we were bonding over our favorite wrestlers, debating their rivalries and practicing their iconic moves during every recess.

Together, we formed an alliance of wrestling enthusiasts and the school hallways echoed with our lively debates and our spirited mimicking of our wrestling heroes. We were unapologetic-ally rowdy, and our excitement occasionally landed us in hot water. DX crotch chops and middle fingers became our signature moves, much to the chagrin of teachers and school staff.

Among those friends, Zach Keyes, Jeremy Cross, Edwin Ocasio, Travis Alt, Casey Brooks and others stood beside me as my unwavering support system. They shared in my journey, encouraged my dreams, and fueled the fire that burned within me. Wrestling became more than just a sport; it was an integral part of who we were and it forged a bond that transcended the confines of our school walls.

Middle school moments: Lunchtime antics with the crew, striking our best wrestling poses.

The wrestling fever that had gripped our group of friends at Woodlake Hills Middle School reached such epic proportions that we found ourselves divided into two stables, each passionately pledging allegiance to a different faction of the nWo. It was as if the Monday Night Wars era had transcended the TV screen and become a daily part of our school curriculum.

On one side, we had the nWo Hollywood faction, donning black and white, strutting with arrogance and causing mischief wherever they went. On the other side stood the nWo Wolfpack supporters, their red and black colors radiating defiance and rebellion. The school hallways became our battlegrounds, with heated debates and playful taunts igniting the rivalry between our two stables.

In the midst of this wrestling-inspired chaos, our good friend Edwin, in a moment of legendary daring, decided to execute a Stone Cold Stunner on a girl classmate, Brittany Jermier. The stunt caught everyone off guard, and while we couldn't help but chuckle at the sheer audacity of it all, it landed Edwin in hot water. The school authorities were not amused, and he found himself suspended for his bold wrestling move.

Despite the consequences, it's a testament to the power of wrestling to inspire us, to bring out our playful spirits, and to forge memories that stand the test of time. While our stables and antics may have caused a bit of trouble along the way, they also brought us closer together as friends. The Monday Night Wars era became more than just a TV spectacle; it became a shared experience that bound us in an unbreakable bond. And even now, as we look back on those days with laughter and fondness, we can't help but feel grateful for the wrestling magic that made our middle school days unforgettable.

Teachers and onlookers could only stand back, bewildered by the spectacle of our clever banter and theatrical showdowns. We were like a hilarious mix of WWE and a comedy club, making every hallway encounter a laugh-out-loud experience.

In the midst of our playful battles, we formed a tight-knit community within the school. The nWo Hollywood and nWo Wolfpack supporters might have seemed like sworn enemies, but underneath it all, we were bonded by the joy of camaraderie and the shared love of laughter.

Those were the days that will forever be etched in our memories. We might not have had championship belts, but our quick wit and sharp tongues were our prized weapons.

In the halls of my middle school, an unexpected bond formed between me and my teacher, Ms. Escobedo. Little did I know that we shared a passion for the world of wrestling, and this common interest would lead to some unforgettable connections.

I was known as a bit of a class clown, but Ms. Escobedo saw beyond my antics. She was a big wrestling fan herself and our conversations would often revolve around what was happening in the wrestling world. It was like finding a kindred spirit in the most unexpected place.

As we exchanged stories and theories about our favorite wrestling stars, our connection grew stronger. Ms. Escobedo's fiance had even begun training to become a wrestler, adding a whole new dimension to our discussions. The itch to get in the ring myself intensified as we dove into the thrilling world of suplexes, body slams and high-flying maneuvers.

In my bedroom, posters of wrestling legends adorned the walls like a shrine to this electrifying sport. Sting, Hogan, the nWo, Flair, Macho Man, Stone Cold, DX and The Rock watched over me as I slept, inspiring dreams of becoming a wrestler someday.

Looking back, I realize that the Monday Night War era of wrestling was truly the pinnacle of excitement. The Rock and Wrestling era of the '80s was remarkable, no doubt, but the Monday Night Wars had something extra - attitude! It was a time when rival wrestling promotions clashed head-to-head on television, creating an epic battle for supremacy. And there I was, a wide-eyed middle school student, witnessing it all unfold as it happened.

The thrill of those evenings, watching wrestling on TV, was unparalleled. Ms. Escobedo and I would chat nonstop about the latest developments, the jaw-dropping surprises and the crazy moments that kept us on the edge of our seats. It wasn't just about the wrestling matches; it was the drama, the storytelling, and the larger-than-life personalities that made it a complete entertainment package.

As I reflect on those years, I feel a surge of gratitude for being a part of that remarkable era. The Monday Night Wars instilled in me a passion for wrestling that has stayed with me through the years. And beyond that, I am grateful for the connection I formed with Ms. Escobedo, who saw past my class clown persona and recognized a fellow wrestling enthusiast.

Those moments in her classroom and our shared excitement for wrestling sparked a friendship that extended beyond the school year. It's amazing how a mutual love for something can create such strong bonds between people. Looking back, I can say with a smile that the Monday Night War era of wrestling was truly a magical time to be a wrestling fan and I am grateful for the memories and connections it brought into my life.

Me, Jeremy (right), Zach (Back) and Jeremy's sister with American Dragon Bryan Danielson when he was at TWA!

As my love for professional wrestling grew, the wrestling scene in San Antonio took an exciting turn with the arrival of WWE legend Shawn Michaels' wrestling promotion, Texas Wrestling Alliance (TWA). It was as if the stars had aligned, bringing the wrestling world even closer to me. The mere thought of seeing wrestling live, just a stone's throw away from home, sent waves of excitement through my entire being.

Every two weeks, like clockwork, I would make my way to the TWA shows, heart pounding with anticipation. The cheers, the boos, the palpable energy in the air—being in the midst of the action was an experience like no other. These shows weren't just entertainment; they were the manifestation of my dreams playing out before my very eyes.

At TWA, I witnessed wrestling greats and rising stars like "Spanky" Brian Kendrick and Bryan Danielson grace the ring with their incredible skills. Their performances left me in awe, their dedication and passion inspiring me to chase my own dreams of becoming a wrestler one day. The allure of the squared circle was magnetic and I knew deep within my heart that I wanted to be part of this exhilarating world. The Texas Wrestling Alliance (TWA), became my gateway to a world of excitement . From the moment I attended my first TWA show I knew I had stumbled upon something extraordinary.

The TWA shows were a melting pot of wrestling brilliance, featuring a diverse array of characters that could rival any big-time wrestling organization. From Rudy "Boy" Gonzalez to the enigmatic Buffet Brothers, to the Wild Ken Johnson and a whole host of other captivating personalities, the TWA roster was a treasure trove of talent.

As I soaked in the electrifying atmosphere at each TWA event I couldn't help but feel an overwhelming sense of excitement and anticipation. Little did I know that I would eventually cross paths with these wrestling icons in the future, not just as a fan, but as a fellow competitor. My passion for the TWA knew no bounds and I soon became a super fan, devouring every bit of news and information about the promotion. I took my enthusiasm to the digital world by creating a dedicated website that covered the latest updates, results, and behind-the-scenes stories of the TWA.

Saturday nights were an eagerly anticipated affair, for that's when after WWE Shotgun Saturday Night, WCW World Wide and WOW Women of

Wrestling, the TWA Total Impact television show would grace our screens. Midnight screenings became a ritual for me, as I meticulously recorded every episode to relive the thrilling moments over and over again. I would find my spot on the couch and enjoy four hours of wrestling every Saturday night.

But the true magic came alive when I stepped foot in the arena where the TWA shows took place. The energy in the air was intense, and I could feel the pulse of excitement coursing through my veins. Eager to secure the best view, I would stand in line for hours, high-tailing it just to snag a prime seat that would put me right in the center of the action. It became a bit of a hang out to wait in the line, where all of us fans built a small little community among ourselves.

Several of us would spend hours outside the venue, eagerly waiting for the chance to grab the best seats. We kind of formed a little community among ourselves. It was me, Zach, Jeremy and even an old man named Ruben, who we affectionately dubbed "Ruben the Cuban." He would usually be ahead of us in line, but occasionally we'd manage to beat him, sparking a friendly competition. As the years went by, Ruben eventually became one of the medics at the local wrestling shows, but that's how I first got to know him.

I have a vivid memory of one particular time when ECW's Sandman was slated to appear. He was a featured wrestler at the event and he surprised us all by actually coming outside to hang out with the fans who had arrived hours early. He chatted with us, posed for photos and it felt incredibly cool. It was a surreal experience to interact with a wrestler we had only seen on TV and it showed a different side of the wrestling world. This was way before the days of selfies and social media, so those photos we took that day are like little treasures, capturing a moment that felt larger than life.

Meeting TV Champion RBG at TWA in 1999.

I've got to share a humorous memory from those early days of waiting in line. One time, my good buddies Jeremy, Zach and I found ourselves at the venue well before showtime. The catch was, there was absolutely nowhere to find a restroom and the situation was getting dire. In an unexpected turn of events, Jeremy had the brilliant idea to play a prank on me – he locked me inside a port a-potty! Looking back, it's one of those stories that always brings a chuckle.

What's even more amusing is that this random port a-potty incident has become a recurring joke between Jeremy and me. Every time we reminisce about those early days of waiting before the shows, this tale inevitably comes up. It's a lighthearted moment that adds to the tapestry of our wrestling journey. So, in honor of Jeremy and the enduring friendship we've shared, I thought it'd be fitting to include this lighthearted anecdote in the pages of this book.

Being a fan of a local wrestling promotion like the TWA was nothing short of amazing. The intimacy and connection with the wrestlers and fellow fans were unparalleled. We were a community bonded by our shared love for this art form, celebrating the spectacle of athleticism and storytelling that unfolded before our eyes.

From the thrilling entrance music to the jaw-dropping moves in the ring, each TWA show was a roller-coaster ride of emotions. It wasn't just a wrestling event; it was an immersive experience that left us on the edge of our seats, cheering for our favorites and sharing in the heartbreak of defeat.

A lot of wrestlers that eventually became huge WWE stars got their starts at the TWA shows, most notably Lance Cade, Brian Kendrick and "American Dragon" Bryan Danielson, who instantly became one of my favorites on the show. He was already technically sound even at an early stage in his career and there was a sense of something special with him.

In addition to that, there was also the Board of Education, Shooter Schultz and several others that made a roster of unique local indy wrestlers that quickly became inspirations for me. It was so much fun to be able to see these shows because it was a regular and more informal setting than what you would see on television.

Zach's birthday party remains one of those memorable moments etched in my mind. It was held at a TWA show, and I distinctly recall the moment during intermission when they called him into the ring to celebrate his birthday. The atmosphere was buzzing with excitement. Little did we know that an unexpected surprise was in store. Suddenly, out of nowhere, Shawn Michaels' iconic theme music blared through the speakers and to our sheer amazement, the Heartbreak Kid himself strode into the ring and personally wished Zach "Happy Birthday".

Jealousy might not quite capture what we all felt at that moment. Here was Zach, right there in the ring with HBK, while the rest of us could only gape in awe from the sidelines. As if to complete the experience, they even pulled off the iconic DX crotch chop. It was a surreal and exhilarating instance that none of us could have anticipated – an unforgettable birthday celebration that had us all caught up in the magic of the wrestling world.

I have to share this other unforgettable memory from those days. One of us managed to win a "Have Dinner with Your Favorite TWA Wrestler" contest. You can bet we all tagged along as a group for this one! The lucky wrestler we chose was none other than Bone Crusher, a formidable figure in the wrestling scene. Sporting an eye-catching orange convict jumpsuit, he had a knack for tossing opponents around in the ring – a true force to be reckoned with.

Sitting down to dinner with Bone Crusher was a surreal experience. We got to dive deep into wrestling conversations with someone who had been right in the middle of the action. We opened up about our aspirations and dreams, sharing our burning desire to become pro wrestlers ourselves someday. It was a rare opportunity to pick the brain of someone who had lived and breathed the world of wrestling, and it only fueled our passion further. The shared enthusiasm and the insightful conversations we had that evening left an indelible mark on us. It was one of those moments that showcased the unique bond forged within the wrestling community – a bond that transcends the roles of fan and wrestler.

I can't help but smile when I reminisce about that evening. Bone Crusher turned out to be incredibly personable and friendly. Not only did he offer us sound advice and encouraging words, but he also had a gift for injecting humor into every conversation. We soaked in every bit of wisdom he shared with us, and his lightheartedness made the experience all the more enjoyable.

Now, here's where it gets interesting – we might have, or might not have, attempted to play matchmakers. You see, we had this idea of setting Bone Crusher up with Zach's older sister. We hoped it might serve as our way to establish a unique connection within the wrestling world.

Ah, the innocence of teenage dreams and schemes! I can't help but chuckle as I reflect on those days. We were a bunch of starry-eyed kids, and the idea of Zach's sister getting romantically involved with one of the pro wrestlers seemed like an audacious yet exciting fantasy. Looking back, it's almost comical how we thought that a sibling's potential love interest could be our ticket to some kind of insider connection in the wrestling world. But hey, we were young and full of imagination, and it just adds to the memories from our time attending all those shows.

"Venom" Paul Diamond held the esteemed title of TWA Champion, and he came with an impressive resume as a former WWE and AWA wrestler. He was the quintessential villain in the Texas Wrestling Alliance, the epitome of a big bad heel that fans loved to hate.

I still remember that unforgettable moment when I crossed paths with Venom in the real world. It was as if the stars aligned that day at the Windsor Park Mall. As I walked into the bustling food court, there he was, Venom himself, seated with his family. My heart skipped a beat – the TWA Champion, right in front of me! I was starstruck and frozen in my tracks, a wrestling fan's dream come true.

Summoning every ounce of courage, I approached Venom, my voice probably shaking with excitement. "Excuse me, Mr. Venom," I managed to stammer, "Could I please have your autograph?" Now, mind you, this wasn't just any autograph request. He was, after all, the embodiment of evil in the TWA wrestling world, and I half expected him to channel his heel persona and turn me down flat.

Me. Jeremy and Travis (right) hanging out in High School

But to my amazement and delight, Venom didn't hesitate. He greeted me with a genuine smile, defying his wrestling character, and accepted my humble napkin as a canvas for his signature. It was a surreal moment, seeing this larger-than-life character off the screen, interacting with his fans in such a down-to-earth manner.

Looking back, I am grateful for the memories and friendships forged during those TWA shows. The passion for wrestling became more than just a hobby; it became a part of my identity. The Texas Wrestling Alliance will forever hold a special place in my heart, where the magic of local wrestling and the thrill of fandom converged, creating memories that will stay with me for a lifetime.

As fate would have it, Shawn Michaels also opened a wrestling school alongside TWA, offering aspiring wrestlers a chance to hone their craft under the guidance of one of the industry's most celebrated performers. It was a golden opportunity, a chance to learn from a living legend. But there was one obstacle standing in my way—I wasn't of age yet. I was only 16 years old and no one under 18 was allowed to train at their facility. I can remember even having my parents personally ask Shawn Michaels mother, who was often at times selling tickets at the TWA events if it was okay for me to train if they gave permission and it was met with a stern "NO". So I had to be regulated to just being a die-hard fan of the product.

I managed to make it to every single TWA show except for one, and the story behind my absence that day is quite a tale. It all started with a rather unexpected and, looking back, quite amusing turn of events.

On that fateful afternoon, my sister and I found ourselves home alone and somehow managed to escalate a regular argument into a full-blown fist fight. Now, I'll admit, my sister has her wild moments, and this was definitely one of them. Picture this: actual plates were flying across the room from the kitchen cabinets, each one shattering as it missed its target (me). But the piece de resistance was when she hurled an unopened three-liter bottle of Sprite straight at my head. It was like something out of a wrestling match, only without the padded ring to soften the impact.

In self-preservation mode, I was doing my best Matrix moves, dodging projectiles and making sure I didn't end up with any accidental facial piercings. At some point, I had to play the referee and put my sister in a makeshift wrestling hold until she cooled off, because at that moment, she was on an absolute rampage.

Finally, I managed to lock myself away in a room, bracing myself for the inevitable grounding that was surely coming my way. And you guessed it, the TWA event that evening was suddenly off the table for me. I couldn't believe my bad luck, especially considering what was lined up for that show – a huge ladder match between American Dragon and Spanky versus the Board of Education: Jeromy Sage and Ruben Cruz for the tag team titles. This was the kind of match that wrestling fans dream of, and there I was, stuck at home.

To add a touch of irony to the situation, I had to wait until the event aired on TV to catch up on the ladder match that I missed out on. As much as it was a frustrating experience back then, looking back now, it's quite the story to tell.

For someone so in love with the world of wrestling, the idea of waiting for my chance to join the wrestling school felt like an eternity. Patience became my ally as I continued to immerse myself in the wrestling world, attending every TWA show and soaking up every moment, all the while eagerly anticipating the day when I would finally be old enough to pursue my dream of stepping into that wrestling school.

From that point on, the days turned into weeks, and the weeks into months, my dedication to wrestling only intensified. I really wanted to train to be a wrestler. My friends, my support system, continued to stand by my side, cheering me on and encouraging me to stay the course. They understood the fire that burned within me, for they too shared the same passion for wrestling that brought us together in the first place.

As we entered the thrilling realm of high school, our passion for wrestling evolved into something even more daring and adventurous. If we weren't old enough to professional wrestle, then we would backyard wrestle. It wasn't the smartest logic seeing that we could have seriously put ourselves in danger, but at the time backyard wrestling was extremely huge on the early internet days.

Back then, WWE seemed to be really pushing the idea that backyard wrestling could be a stepping stone to success, especially when they talked about Mick Foley and The Hardy Boyz and their backyard wrestling experiences. Being teenagers, we thought,

"Hey, this is the way to go if we want to make it big in wrestling." I can't even count how many times we watched that clip of Mick Foley jumping off his garage on Monday Night Raw. That image is stuck in my memory.

Seeing Foley take that daring leap left a strong impression on me. The whole scene—the crazy move, the insane landing on the mattress—it's something I can't forget. At the time, it felt like Foley's leap embodied the essence of wrestling, that boldness and fervor that made us want to be part of it all. It made us believe that backyard wrestling was our shot at following in our heroes' footsteps.

Back then, we didn't really grasp the risks and challenges that came with backyard wrestling. We were drawn to the spectacle, the idea of imitating our wrestling idols, and the hope that this could be our ticket into the wrestling world. WWE talking about Foley and The Hardy Boyz doing it only added to our conviction that this was the way to go.

With our hearts set on creating our own wrestling legacy, we took the plunge and founded our own backyard wrestling promotion: the Hardcore Wrestling Federation (HWF). Every weekend became an adrenaline-fueled adventure as we fearlessly performed moves on each other, creating our own epic matches that defied the boundaries of imagination.

With a mix of excitement and trepidation, we set up our events in Travis backyard and used our imagination to transform it into an arena of spectacle and drama. Clad in our makeshift wrestling gear, we channeled the spirit of our wrestling heroes, crafting our own larger-than-life personas that were sure to entertain. We even had regular attendees of friends and family come watch us.

In the Hardcore Wrestling Federation, we pushed our boundaries and tested our limits, executing high-flying maneuvers and devastating finishers with reckless abandon. The thrill of each match was heightened by the knowledge that we were not professional wrestlers, but the love for this adrenaline-pumping spectacle drove us to take risks and create unforgettable moments.

Amid the daring escapades of the HWF, Travis's house became our hallowed battleground. With his father often away, we saw an opportunity to transform the yard into our own personal wrestling arena. Every weekend, we'd gather with unbridled excitement, ready to unleash our high-flying moves and fearless stunts.

However, our adrenaline-fueled wrestling extravaganza didn't come without its challenges. Travis's father had little tolerance for our antics, especially when they involved diving off the roof or mimicking the infamous Stone Cold getting hit by a car.

Yes, we had the brilliant idea of using Edwin's car to hit Travis in what we thought was a near perfect replication of Rikishi hitting Stone Cold Steve Austin with the car when he "did it for The Rock". Unfortunately, we had bad timing with it, because Travis' father witnessed the whole ordeal and threw a heavy duty flashlight right at Edwin's car destroying the back window.

Me and Steven aka Hardcore Rican (right) wrestling in HWF

So, whenever we heard his father's car pulling up the driveway, panic would ensue, and we'd scatter like a flock of startled birds. Because to be honest, he was super scary, didn't talk to any of us and we didn't want to get on his bad side despite Travis assuring us that all was okay to wrestle. We were just kids being kids.

Despite our best efforts to make a quick getaway, Travis's father would sometimes catch us in the act. He'd appear with a stern look that signaled it was time to disperse and cease our daredevilry. His disapproval was understandable, but in the heat of the moment, our youthful enthusiasm often overruled our sense of caution.

In retrospect, I acknowledge that our actions could have resulted in much worse consequences, and Travis's father's reaction was a clear message to temper our enthusiasm and ensure our safety. It was a lesson learned, albeit in a memorable and somewhat comical way.

The backyard wrestling was my way of trying to get my foot in the door in any way possible. I was too young to train at the Shawn Michaels Academy which is where I was determined to go once I was of age. I had this wild idea that just like Mick Foley and the Hardy Boyz, I would immediately be ready when the time came to become a part of this business. So I attempted to be patient.

Aside from the ridiculous backyard wrestling shenanigans, my high school experience at Judson High School in Converse, Texas, was a mix of excitement and challenges, as I was both in football and wrestling. However, I couldn't ignore the fact that I was a 5'6" and 105 lb little guy, which made it tough for me to excel in these sports.

Playing football and being part of the wrestling team were exhilarating, and the chumminess among teammates was heartwarming. But my physical stature posed a significant hurdle. I was well aware that I wasn't the strongest or the biggest player on the field or on the mat. Aside from that, I absolutely loved high school. I was friends with everyone and still am friends with a lot of people from back then to this day.

As I stepped onto the football field, usually towered over by teammates, I often felt like an underdog in a world of giants. My size and lack of strength were apparent, and it was challenging to compete against bigger, more powerful athletes.

Similarly, when I joined the wrestling team, I faced the same struggles. My opponents in my weight class were often much stronger, and it was tough to match their physical prowess. Despite my dedication and hard work, I couldn't achieve the same level of success as some of my teammates.

Looking back, I have to confess I was a bit of a wallflower when it came to anything remotely athletic. Practicing and actively participating? Nah, not my jam. During football practice, I'd gravitate toward this ragtag bunch of guys who, like me, weren't the shining stars of the team. Instead of honing our skills, we'd spend the whole practice cracking jokes and chit chatting about pro wrestling.

Looking back, I wish I had taken things a tad more seriously, but truth be told, I was timid and a bit fearful. I wasn't exactly the poster child for athleticism —I was one of the slowpokes on the team, and if we're talking about weightlifting, I might have qualified as one of the weakest links. Suffice to say, I got left in the dust pretty darn quickly.

My high school didn't have a wrestling team throughout its existence, until my sophomore year when things finally changed. I was quite thrilled about this development because you always hear about how some of the world's top pro wrestlers honed their skills through amateur wrestling.

I had hoped that this experience would be a stepping stone on my journey towards becoming a professional wrestler. My focus was on building a solid resume before even considering a wrestling school. I figured that anyone willing to train me would see the determination and seriousness I had about being an athlete.

I found myself in the 145 weight class. Given that wrestling was more of an individual sport compared to the team dynamics of football, standing out became a tougher feat. My class had a mix of individuals ranging from guys with shorter and stockier builds like myself to tall and muscular ones. I distinctly recall one particular moment when I had an exhibition match against my friend Travis. This was one of the rare instances I stepped onto the mat. My nerves were through the roof, and as I approached the mat, I could clearly hear my mother's voice yelling, "Travis, you better not hurt my little boy!" The entire gym erupted into laughter, and in that moment, I felt incredibly small and wished I wasn't there.

Travis and I got down to wrestling, but my stamina only held up for a couple of minutes before he easily overpowered me. I'll be honest, my skills were far from impressive. Despite that, I was determined to attend wrestling practice every day, even though I was juggling a full-time job. Often, I'd have to head straight to work right after practice, and my weekends were usually occupied by work commitments too. Despite the challenges, I gave it my all, and I have to admit, the regular practice did wonders for my fitness. If there's one thing I wish I could rewind time for, it's giving a bit more seriousness to wrestling at school. In hindsight, I've come to realize that collegiate-style wrestling is an excellent sport for character development.

I still recall the chance I had to step into a varsity match due to an injured competitor in my weight class. At the last minute, though, he decided to play hardball and challenged me for the spot. He was much more athletic and built than I was, and honestly, he wiped the floor with me. I didn't even stand a chance. It would've been nice if he had simply allowed me the opportunity, as even a loss would've contributed toward my chances of earning a Letterman's jacket. But, hey, such is life, right?

I had a blast in high school! Miss those days!

Looking back, I can honestly say I had a good time during my high school years. I didn't exactly fit into any particular category; I wasn't a nerd nor a jock. I found myself somewhere in between, connecting with friends from various groups in school. Surprisingly, I had a fair share of girls I'd chat with at school, so I guess you could say I was somewhat popular.

Admittedly, though, there were times when I coasted through my classes. It wasn't that I was a lazy student, but rather that I lacked the focus I should've had. I'd often find myself engrossed in conversations with classmates or attempting to catch some Z's during those early morning classes, given that our school day started at a groggy 7:15 am. Adding to the mix, I worked at the Galaxy movie theater, frequently keeping me there past midnight during the week. The combination of work and late nights meant I was always exhausted, and once home, I'd waste away the hours online or playing video games. So, it's safe to say my time management skills were far from stellar.

During my teenage years, I drew inspiration from pro wrestlers like Mick Foley, who defied expectations and proved that size wasn't the sole determinant of success. Foley's tenacity and resilience served as a beacon of hope, reminding me that being an underdog didn't mean I was destined to fail.

I was engrossed in reading Mick Foley's captivating book, "Have a Nice Day: A Tale of Blood and Sweat socks." Foley's personal journey, chronicled within those pages, resonated with me deeply. Much like me, he was a high school student harboring an unwavering determination to carve a path into the world of professional wrestling. As I pored over his words, I found myself connecting with his experiences on a profound level.

In tandem with Foley's book, WWE was weaving a narrative that beautifully captured his profound love for the wrestling business. The storytelling was so masterful that it didn't merely entertain; it inspired me to the core. Mick Foley's story became more than just ink on pages; it became a guiding light for my own aspirations, serving as a constant reminder that dreams, no matter how ambitious, were worth pursuing.

I can vividly recall the surge of inspiration that surged through me as I flipped through the pages of Mick Foley's book. His trials, his triumphs, and his sheer determination painted a clear picture of what it took to make it in the wrestling world. And that picture was one that I held close as I navigated the halls of my high school and the early mornings of training.

Mick Foley's journey wasn't just his own; it became a part of mine too. His story wove its way into my identity as a wrestler-in-training, offering hope and motivation when the road seemed steep. Looking back, I realize that his book and WWE's portrayal of his passion were more than sources of entertainment; they were catalysts that fueled my fire.

I got to personally thank Foley in 2008 for being my inspiration.

Through every triumph and setback I experienced, in my pursuit. And as the clock ticked closer to the day of my age eligibility for the wrestling school, I knew that the moment I had longed for was drawing near. The wait was soon to be over, and I would finally have the chance to chase my dreams with the same determination that had guided me from the very beginning.

Pro wrestling consumed every fiber of my being, seeping into every moment of my waking life.

Whether I was working at the Galaxy movie theater or sweating it out on the football field during high school practice, my mind was fixated on this electrifying world of pro wrestling. Even to this day over 30 years later, my father and I tune in every Monday night to watch wrestling. It became an all-encompassing obsession, a burning passion that fueled my every thought and action.

In the middle of my daily routine, I found myself consumed by all things wrestling. If I wasn't watching the latest wrestling matches, I was immersing myself in the pages of wrestling magazines, soaking up every bit of knowledge and insight. There was no escape from this captivating world, nor did I desire one.

Being part of the wrestling business wasn't just a dream for me—it was a calling, a purpose that I yearned to fulfill. I knew I wasn't the biggest or the strongest person out there, but my heart and soul were dedicated to making an impact in this industry. I believed with unwavering conviction that I had the passion and determination to carve out something special, even if it meant succeeding at the local level.

The TWA shows served as an inspiration like no other. Witnessing the magic and dedication of the wrestlers in that ring ignited a fire within me, a desire to be part of something greater than myself. Every cheer from the crowd, every high-flying maneuver and every heartfelt promo spoke directly to my soul, fueling my pursuit of this dream.

Chapter 2
Bumping with Beanie Babies:
Learning to Wrestle

One fateful night, as I absentmindedly watched the news, a local segment caught my attention. The reporter ventured into the realms of the unknown, exploring various attractions in town. Little did I know that this seemingly ordinary segment would lead me to an extraordinary discovery - a local wrestling show by the name of American Championship Wrestling.

I was taken aback, realizing there was more to the wrestling scene in town than I had ever imagined. The reporter showcased a group of skilled wrestlers, all led by the imposing figure of a bodybuilder named

Prince Fontenot. As I watched the segment I was amazed as they performed jaw-dropping moves and bumps inside the squared circle. But that wasn't all – the segment revealed that this wrestling promotion had something I had been searching for – a wrestling school near me.

A spark ignited within me as I contemplated the possibilities. Another wrestling school presented itself as an opportunity, and I couldn't resist the urge to find out more. With eager anticipation, I dialed the number provided and inquired if they accepted students under the age of 18. To my delight, they did welcome young aspiring wrestlers like me with open arms.

Sure, it wasn't the Shawn Michaels Wrestling Academy, but it was a start somewhere. I told myself once I was of age I would still enroll at Shawn Michaels' school to further my craft, but for now I would take what I could get.

With excitement coursing through my veins, I couldn't wait to share the incredible news with my friends. We had always been in this together, and this opportunity was too thrilling to keep to myself. So, I dialed their phone numbers and animatedly told them about the wrestling school at the Texas Hideaway Flea

Market – a chance to step into a real wrestling ring and live out our dreams.

As we chatted, a mixture of nerves and excitement surfaced. It wasn't an easy decision for everyone, but two of my closest friends, Zach and Travis, stood tall beside me, ready to embrace the challenge with the same fervor and determination. Their unwavering support and bravery solidified our decision to take this plunge together.

My heart raced with joy as I realized that my dream of becoming a wrestler was within reach. The next morning, training awaited me, promising an adventure that would change the course of my life. Sleep evaded me that night; my excitement reached unparalleled heights. The thought of stepping foot into the wrestling world, learning the ropes and honing my skills consumed my every thought.

As the morning sun painted the sky with hues of gold, I found myself standing outside the "school" that would soon become the stage for my dreams. It wasn't a conventional training facility, not even close to the grandeur of the famed Shawn Michaels school I had heard about. No, this was a corner at the Texas Hideaway Flea Market, large enough to house a wrestling ring and a place where my dreams would finally take flight.

As I gazed upon the modest setup, a mixture of excitement and nervous anticipation surged through my veins. It didn't matter that this wrestling school was different from what I had envisioned; what truly mattered was the chance to step inside a wrestling ring for the very first time.

Prince Fontenot

The moment I stepped through those makeshift ropes, a world of possibilities opened up before me.

The creaking of the ropes, the smell of the canvas, and the prospect of what was to come enveloped me. I knew this was just the beginning of an unforgettable journey.

Meeting Prince Fontenot was an awe-inspiring experience that left me both intimidated and intrigued. A hulking African American dude, he stood tall with a physique that could only be described as larger than life. As a bodybuilder, he exuded strength and power, making me wonder if he'd effortlessly throw us around during training. But to my surprise, Prince was anything but intimidating when he introduced himself. Beneath his imposing exterior lay a kind and welcoming soul. He proudly revealed himself as the owner and operator of ACW, the wrestling promotion that had caught my attention.

As my friends and I met the rest of the ACW crew, we were greeted with warmth and camaraderie. Juliano Smooth, Aztlan King, Lightning Jay, Tank, and Eurocane – they were the homegrown ACW talent, a tight-knit group who worked together at Luby's restaurant. They were not only talented wrestlers but also shared a quirky sense of humor that filled the room with laughter.

Juliano Smooth was the epitome of cool, a smooth talker who could fire off witty remarks about anyone at a moment's notice, catching you off guard and leaving you chuckling. This charisma translated seamlessly into his in-ring and promo work, and you could sense his potential brimming beneath the surface. Then there was Lightning Jay, the masked wonder, who may have hidden his face, but not his heart and determination. He poured his soul into every practice and every move in the ring. A truly genuine person, always with a smile on his face, he exemplified the spirit of wrestling.

Aztlan King, well, he carried a certain cocky demeanor, to be frank. Our interactions were sparse, but I did recognize his solid skills and willingness to lend a helping hand when I was still finding my footing. He played a role in laying my wrestling foundation, and for that I'm grateful.

Eurocane, however, was a whole different breed. He commanded respect, a seasoned veteran whose wisdom was sought after by all. He assumed the mantle of leadership with ease, a guiding force for us all, offering advice that came from years of hard-earned experience.

And then, of course, there was Tommy "Tank" Hemphill. Oh, Tank, a wild intimidating presence with an even bigger heart. He was a walking contradiction – a huggable teddy bear with a short fuse. If you were in his circle of care, he would stand as your protector against all odds. His wit was matched only by his strength, and he had a talent for making even the toughest days feel a little lighter with his humor.

Tommy "The Tank" Hemphill

Our wrestling training sessions had an unusual schedule, and the reason behind it was quite unique. The ACW guys, who were also part of the training, had commitments at their job when it opened for business. Since they worked at Luby's, breakfast time was mandatory for them to be there. This practical constraint meant that the early mornings on weekends were the only available time for us to train. While I was accustomed to waking up at the crack of dawn for school every weekday, adapting to early weekend starts presented a whole new challenge.

My daily routine of catching the bus at 5:30 am was almost a ritual, but waking up early on weekends added a new layer to the equation. The familiar sound of the alarm clock on school days now echoed on Saturdays and Sundays too, demanding my groggy body to rise and shine. Yet, within this adjustment, there was a silver lining that defined the extraordinary commitment of my father. As I ventured into the world of wrestling, my father stood steadfastly by my side. Amid the early morning haze, he offered unwavering support and encouragement.

It's these quiet moments that truly reveal the depth of a parent's love and dedication. While the world slept, my father and I embarked on those early morning drives, an unspoken pact formed between us. Through his presence, my father taught me a powerful lesson – the value of dedication, hard work and the lengths to which a parent will go to nurture their child's dreams.

At that time, my father held down a demanding full-time job as an immigration officer. His schedule offered him just two precious days of respite each week – Saturdays and Sundays. Yet, despite his own commitments and limited free time, my father wholeheartedly committed himself to my dream. Every practice session, he would wake up alongside me at the crack of dawn, a testament to his unwavering dedication.

I can still picture those early mornings, as the sun barely cast its first rays on the horizon, my father and I would embark on our journey across town. His presence in the car, waiting patiently during my wrestling practices, was a silent affirmation of his unbreakable support. It's these moments that truly define a parent's love – the willingness to sacrifice personal comfort for the sake of their child's aspirations.

Reflecting on those times, I am profoundly grateful for my father's sacrifices. His encouragement and dedication were never in short supply. Through the cold early mornings and the long waits, he offered me a precious gift: his time, his firm presence, and his faith in my dreams. It's a debt of gratitude that can never truly be repaid, but one that serves as a constant reminder of the power of a parent's love and support.

Despite the challenges of juggling school, a full-time job at the Galaxy movie theater till midnight on Fridays and Saturdays, and early morning training, my determination to become a wrestler never wavered. The passion that had ignited within me when I first watched wrestling on that fateful night fueled my drive to pursue this dream, no matter the sacrifices. It was now go time.

This was my moment, all of the dreaming to become a professional wrestler, tuning into wrestling on television every chance I could, wrestling in the backyard, doing wrestling in high school, was all leading to this very moment. I was finally in a wrestling ring and I was set to become the next big star.

In the heart of that wrestling ring, I stood with a surge of excitement coursing through my veins. In my mind's eye, I could already hear the deafening chants of the crowd, cheering my name. The moment had arrived – our warm-up began, encompassing stretches, mat drills and rolls. But the highlight of the day was yet to come – it was time for me to take my first back bump.

For those unfamiliar with wrestling lingo, the back bump is the holy grail of wrestling fundamentals. It's often humorously referred to as "learning to fall," but its importance cannot be overstated. Without mastering this skill, every other move in wrestling becomes impossible to execute safely.

Nervous but eager to conquer this pivotal moment, I stepped into the center of the ring. With a deep breath, I prepared to take the back bump. I closed my eyes, clenched my fist and was ready for it. Little did I know that this seemingly simple move would prove to be a formidable challenge.

As I fell back, an instant rush of pain surged through me. My head hit the mat with a jolt, and I saw stars. The impact had been much harder than I had anticipated, and the whiplash from the fall sent shock waves of pain through the back of my head.

Summoning my determination, I shook off the discomfort and tried again. BOOM! The impact of the second attempt echoed through my skull, leaving me reeling. But I refused to be deterred. I got back up and attempted once more. BOOM! Another painful collision with the mat.

Tears welled up in my eyes as the pain became unbearable. I couldn't ignore it any longer. My dreams of conquering the wrestling world seemed momentarily shattered as the agony overwhelmed me. As I stood in the ring, my heart pounding with nerves and determination, little did I know that this moment would become a pivotal turning point in my wrestling journey. Prince and the other wrestlers had ordered me to step out of the ring and watch the rest of the practice – an immediate blow to my spirits. Defeat washed over me as I struggled to comprehend why I couldn't get the hang of that seemingly simple back bump.

The next two weeks proved to be a relentless battle with frustration and pain. Every practice, I attempted the back bump, and every time, the impact sent shock waves of agony through the back of my head. I couldn't grasp the proper technique, and it began to gnaw at my confidence. Doubts crept in, and I started questioning whether wrestling was truly meant for me.

Two weeks of grappling with self-doubt and pain took its toll. I was ready to throw in the towel, convinced that perhaps wrestling wasn't my calling. As the next practice loomed, I knew it was going to be my last. The gathering was set to take place at Prince's house due to the cold weather, and the ring mats were laid out on his living room floor. This arrangement meant there was no cushioning like a typical ring would provide – every bump would be harsh and unforgiving.

As we sat in a circle, conversation naturally veered towards my struggles with the back bump. Just as I was about to express my doubts, Prince intervened. He asked me to step onto the mat in the center of his living room. Intrigued yet apprehensive, I followed his instruction. What came next would change everything.

With a beanie baby in hand, Prince demonstrated a simple yet profound adjustment. He asked me to tuck the beanie baby under my chin and hold it tightly as I fell back. I took a deep breath, put the beanie baby in place, and braced for impact. This time, as I fell back, something miraculous happened – I landed perfectly on the mat with no pain. It was as if the weight of the world had been lifted off my shoulders.

In that instant, I realized that it wasn't wrestling that wasn't for me; it was merely a matter of unlocking the right technique. Prince's simple yet ingenious suggestion had made all the difference. The beanie baby served as a reminder to tuck my chin and protect my head during the fall. With that small adjustment, I had triumphed over my own doubts and conquered the hurdle that had seemed insurmountable.

A lot of what being in wrestling is about, is how you react and adapt to situations. This was the first of many times in my wrestling experience that I learned quitting right away is not always the answer. Sometimes sticking with your heart and proving yourself and others wrong goes a long way. But it also takes trusting those who believe in you. Even if they come across as tough on you, if they didn't care they wouldn't push you beyond your limits. Prince was the first person, out of many, to really show me what tough love was in the wrestling business.

From that moment on, I approached each practice with renewed determination and passion. Wrestling had challenged me, tested me, and made me question my abilities, but I had emerged stronger than ever. That beanie baby became my good luck charm, a symbol of victory, and a constant reminder that perseverance and guidance could transform obstacles into stepping stones. As I continued my journey as a wrestler, I carried that lesson in my heart, knowing that even in the face of adversity, I had the strength to rise and conquer.

But wrestling is about more than just mastering moves; it's about resilience, determination, and pushing past your limits. Despite the pain and frustration, I knew that giving up was not an option. With a heavy heart, I swallowed my pride and sought the guidance of my trainers, determined to perfect this critical skill. Can you imagine how different my life would have been if I had quit? I know I would have definitely regretted it.

As the days turned into weeks, training at the ACW school progressed at a breakneck pace. Time seemed to fly by as we honed our skills, taking body slams, executing dropkicks and perfecting suplexes. Everything was falling into place, and it felt like my dreams of becoming a wrestler were finally taking shape.

But just as we settled into our newfound rhythm, a wave of change washed over our training regimen. Three newcomers arrived from the renowned Shawn Michaels Wrestling Academy, which had rebranded to the Texas Wrestling Academy. Spiro, Slayer and The UK Kid were their names, each bringing a unique set of skills and experience.

Spiro and Slayer, two impressive figures with face paint reminiscent of the rock band KISS, were powerhouses in the making. On the other hand, The UK Kid was a technical marvel, having already wrestled back home in England despite being only two years older than me. Their arrival signified a shift in our training approach, and the once laid-back vibe gave way to a more intense and disciplined environment.

These seasoned wrestlers took one look at our training routine and knew that it was time to raise the bar. The days of easy-going practice sessions were over. Instead, they introduced us to grueling blow-up drills intended to push us to our limits and beyond. For someone like me, who wasn't naturally gifted athletically, these drills were a daunting challenge.

From squats to crunches, from push-ups to running a mile, there was no time out. We had to do all this before even stepping into the ring, and exhaustion was our constant companion. At times, the drills were so demanding that I questioned whether I could endure them. But as the days passed, I began to witness a transformation – not just in my physical conditioning but also in my mental fortitude.

Zach and Travis, my fellow comrades on this wrestling journey, were making remarkable strides in their training. In fact, their progress was impressive, often matching my own pace. We were a trio fueled by shared dreams, each pushing ourselves to the limits to grasp a future in professional wrestling. However, a twist of fate intervened, and Travis, the once-determined aspiring wrestler, suddenly vanished from the scene, leaving behind an unexplained void.

Yet, despite Travis's unexpected departure, the bond between Zach and me persisted. Having one of my closest friends by my side during those intense training sessions eased the weight of the grueling path we had chosen. Zach's unwavering presence transformed the sweat-soaked mats of the training facility into a realm of mutual support, where we leaned on each other's determination to keep moving forward.

It's worth noting that Zach and I weren't exempt from the struggles that came with this pursuit. The path to becoming a professional wrestler was laden with challenges that tested not only our physical endurance but also our mental fortitude. Wrestling training demanded an unyielding commitment, relentless practice and an ability to persevere in the face of obstacles. Zach, like me, grappled with moments of doubt and exhaustion. But in those moments, the shared experience and our friendship acted as anchors, propelling us past the hurdles.

The journey we undertook was anything but easy. It required resilience, dedication and the tenacity to weather setbacks. While Travis's departure was a setback, the bond Zach and I shared grew even stronger, an embodiment of the kind of friendship forged through shared ambitions and challenges.

Under the guidance of Spiro, Slayer and The UK Kid, we learned to push ourselves beyond what we thought was possible. These men became more than just trainers; they became mentors who instilled in us the determination and work ethic required to thrive in the world of wrestling. Training with those three studs was nothing short of grueling; their commitment to shaping us into formidable wrestlers knew no bounds. There were moments that brought both humor and hard lessons. One incident, in particular, stands out as a hilarious attempt to sidestep training.

The weather was abysmal, and we concocted an excuse to the UK Kid that setting up the ring might be futile due to the impending rain. Hoping to have an easy day or maybe skip training altogether, we were presented with a choice—practice or go home. We couldn't risk seeming not serious about our wrestling aspirations, so we proposed a "brilliant" idea—why not just have a cardio day with basic calisthenics?

Unfortunately, our attempt to outsmart UK Kid didn't go as planned. He had a chip on his shoulder from the early wake-up call and our reluctance to set up the ring. So, instead of a light cardio session, we found ourselves enduring 10 sets of 50 squats, 10 sets of 25 push-ups, 10 sets of 25 crunches, followed by a two-mile run. It was a punishing lesson in humility and perseverance.

Through gritted teeth and burning muscles, we completed the grueling routine. When UK Kid asked if we had any comments or concerns, one of my fellow students, with equal parts frustration and jest, candidly remarked, "Yes, I think you are an asshole." We immediately busted out laughing, even UK couldn't contain the reaction.

As tough as that practice was, it left a lasting impression. We learned that trying to avoid training had consequences and that the UK Kid was not one to be trifled with. But beyond the sweat and soreness, these moments of challenge brought us closer together. The comradery formed during those arduous sessions became the bedrock of our wrestling brotherhood.

Reflecting on that day, I can't help but smile. It was a reminder that dedication to our craft was paramount, and taking the hard road was often the best path to growth. UK Kid's tough love taught us valuable lessons that extended beyond the wrestling ring, molding us into disciplined individuals with an tenacious passion for the sport.

In the annals of my wrestling journey, this day remains a vivid memory. Through the laughter and sweat, UK Kid proved to be a mentor who pushed us to be our best selves and to embrace the challenges that came with pursuing our dreams in the world of professional wrestling.

At the time I thought it was a blessing in disguise to be shown the ins and outs by three individuals who were actually in the wrestling school that I had dreamed of being a part of. I felt it was going to put me ahead of the curb in regards to preparation for a more authentic wrestling school like the Shawn Michaels Wrestling Academy.

The road to success was paved with sweat, sore muscles and moments of doubt, but we embraced the challenge. The blow-up drills may have been tough, but they shape us into wrestlers with the resilience to face any obstacle head-on. Looking back, I credit these three men as the ones who molded me into the wrestler I am today, teaching me that hard work, dedication, and a willingness to push past my limits were the keys to unlocking my true potential in the squared circle.

As we immersed ourselves in the ACW family, I felt a sense of belonging that was both comforting and exhilarating. The ACW guys welcomed us with open arms, embracing us as part of their tight-knit circle. Their humor, friendship, and genuine support made the early mornings and long hours worthwhile. In the wrestling world, we found more than just a sport – we found a family of like-minded individuals who shared the same love for the art of wrestling. And together, we were determined to create something extraordinary in that modest corner of the Texas Hideaway Flea Market.

Despite the unconventional setting, the passion and dedication of the trainers and fellow aspiring wrestlers quickly became evident. We were a group of individuals united by a shared dream, driven to learn, grow, and excel in the art of wrestling. The unorthodox location only added to the charm, as it emphasized the raw and grassroots essence of our pursuit.

Looking back, I realize that it wasn't the lavishness of the facility that mattered, but the heart and soul that we poured into our training. In that modest corner of the flea market, I found the courage to chase my dreams relentlessly, knowing that the journey might be unconventional, but the destination would be nothing short of extraordinary.

The wrestling ring at the Texas Hideaway Flea Market became a symbol of hope and possibility for me, a place where I could let go of inhibitions and become the wrestler I had always aspired to be. The path I had chosen might have been where I wanted to be, but it was uniquely mine, and I wouldn't have had it any other way. This was my introduction to the world of wrestling and I was ready to embrace it with all the passion and dedication in my heart.

Chapter 3
Lights, Camera, Action:
The Debut Match

One day at the ACW training facility, an unexpected announcement sent my heart racing with a potent mixture of excitement and nerves. I was told that I would be wrestling at ACW's highly anticipated 1-year anniversary show on March 3rd, 2001. The news caught me completely off guard – I had only started training in January, and I never imagined I would progress this quickly. Looking back, I now realize that I was far from ready, but in that moment, I was determined to embrace the opportunity with all my might.

The thought of stepping into the ring in front of a live audience, just a few months after starting my training, was both exhilarating and daunting. Doubts swirled in my mind, questioning whether I could rise to the occasion. However, Prince's firm belief in my potential bolstered my confidence. He saw something in me, something worth showcasing on that special night, and that trust gave me a profound sense of gratitude and responsibility.

Prince, the guiding force behind ACW, was more than just a wrestling mentor; he became a mentor in life. He took me under his wing, recognizing my passion for the sport and my eagerness to learn. His encouragement and constructive feedback pushed me to test my limits, to go beyond what I thought was possible, and to show the world what I was truly capable of.

With the support and guidance of Prince and the other experienced wrestlers at ACW, I immersed myself in learning every aspect of professional wrestling. Every training session became an opportunity to refine my skills, hone my technique, and perfect my performance. I pushed myself harder than ever before, knowing that this was my chance to make a lasting impression on the wrestling world.

The biggest change for me was that I was no longer focused on my hobbies and activities in high school, such as football and even wrestling on the school team. I was a hundred percent focused on being a pro wrestler, and even my grades took a backseat. This was all I had wanted to do, there was no backup plan.

One of the only photos from my first match, I am in the ring nervous!

The weeks leading up to the event were a whirlwind of emotions – a potent blend of nerves and excitement. Prince took charge of preparing Jay and me for the match, meticulously guiding us through the process. In addition to the wrestling preparation, I was given a unique directive – I needed to get a black karate gi and some face paint to conceal my youthful appearance and create a more imposing wrestling persona.

As the momentous night finally arrived, I stood backstage, adrenaline coursing through my veins. The arena buzzed with anticipation, and the air was electric with excitement. The sight of the crowd, a sea of eager faces, sent a surge of nerves and exhilaration through my entire body. This was it – the culmination of months of hard work and dedication.

As my entrance music echoed through the arena, signaling my moment to shine, I made my way to the ring. But just before I stepped out, like the scene in the first Tobey Maguire Spider-Man movie, the ring announcer approached me with an unexpected question – what name did I want to be called? My mind raced, desperately searching for something that would embody the essence of my wrestling persona. Suddenly, the name "Dark Spectre" flashed in my mind, and I blurted it out without hesitation.

The ring announcer, however, had other ideas. He suggested "The Spectre" instead, and with little time to think, I agreed. Being a rookie, I didn't feel like I had much say in the matter, and I was just grateful for the opportunity to be in that ring.

Stepping through the ropes, the canvas of the wrestling ring felt like hallowed ground, connecting me to the world of professional wrestling. It was a surreal moment of realization that I was about to live out a dream I had nurtured for years. Every inch of the ring held significance as it represented countless hours of training and preparation.

My first opponent: Lightning Jay

My opponent, Lightning Jay, approached the ring with a determined look in his eyes. Despite being new to wrestling like me, he had a raw energy and talent that made him a formidable opponent. As we faced each other in the ring, the tension was intense. We were both rookies, eager to prove ourselves and show the world what we were made of.

The match itself, though brief, was executed smoothly, thanks to our precise preparation. Each move and sequence played out like a carefully choreographed dance. We worked together seamlessly, making the most of our limited experience to deliver an engaging and entertaining performance. It was not a classic by any means, but to this 16 year old kid, it might as well have been my WrestleMania moment.

The memory of my first match with Lightning Jay is etched into my mind with vivid clarity. Every move, every moment, and every emotion are as fresh as if it happened just yesterday. Even though it's been over two decades since that unforgettable day in 2001, the magic of that match still lingers, making it one of the best days of my life.

As soon as the bell rang, the adrenaline surged through my veins as Lightning Jay and I locked up in the center of the ring. With a swift spin, I took control and executed a powerful arm drag, followed by a snap mare into a thunderous leg drop. As I rose to my feet,

I couldn't resist the urge to taunt the crowd, boldly declaring that Lightning Jay had nothing on me.

With momentum on my side, I whipped Lightning Jay across the ring, only for him to counter with a slick Sunset flip, catching me off guard. The referee's hand came down for a two-count, but I quickly cut him off, regaining my composure.

With determination in my eyes, I strategically worked my way into the corner, delivering a series of impactful strikes to Lightning Jay. In an impressive display of athleticism, I shot him off into the ropes, setting him up for a move that would secure my dominance.

However, as fate would have it, I walked right into his devastating Diamond Cutter - a move that took me completely by surprise. Before I knew it, Lightning Jay capitalized on the moment, swiftly covering me for the three-count. The crowd erupted for the scrappy little baby face getting the best of "The Spectre" that night.

Though I didn't emerge as the victor, the overwhelming joy of having taken that courageous step into the spotlight overshadowed any disappointment. The match may have been scripted, but the elation and pride I felt were genuine. As we received applause and cheers from the audience, the sense of accomplishment was indescribable. I had faced my fears and stepped into the ring, making my mark in the world of professional wrestling, or at least at the Texas Hideaway Flea Market.

I'd also like to point out that this match was only a minute and 42 seconds long, but all the days, weeks and months leading up to me achieving this goal made it the best minute and 42 seconds of my life. Anytime I bring up the story of my first match, I always tell everyone how short it was and it is often met with laughs. Sure, it is funny to hear, but that minute and 42 seconds was earned through blood, sweat and tears.

As I made my way backstage, a mixture of emotions overwhelmed me. While my debut match may have been brief, the significance of the moment wasn't lost on me. As I stepped behind the curtain, I was met with the warm congratulations of my wrestling peers in the locker room. And after the show, my friends and family waited by my car. Their beaming smiles and heartfelt applause conveyed a message louder than any words could express – I had already succeeded in their eyes, and that meant the world to me.

The moment my friends from middle school gathered around me, eager to capture a photo of me in my wrestling gear and ask for my first-ever wrestling autographs, was nothing short of magical. It was a core memory that touched my heart deeply, and I know it will remain with me until my very last breath. The significance of that moment extended far beyond the joy of achieving a personal milestone; it symbolized the unwavering support and camaraderie we shared over our mutual love for pro wrestling.

That night, I learned a valuable lesson about the power of passion and determination. My first wrestling match was not just about the outcome; it was about the journey, the experience, and the sense of accomplishment that came with stepping into that ring. It taught me that sometimes, the true victory lies in the courage to chase one's dreams, regardless of the immediate results.

Years have passed since that pivotal moment in my wrestling journey, yet the memories of that night fill me with a rush of nostalgia. It was a time of humble beginnings, where I stepped into the unknown with a mix of fear and determination. Little did I know that the journey that started that night would become a profound and cherished part of my life, filled with a roller-coaster of highs and lows, triumphs, and setbacks.

In hindsight, that first match at the 1-year anniversary show meant more than just the outcome. It was a testament to the passion and dedication that propelled me forward, even when uncertainty loomed on the horizon. But it wasn't just about me; it was about the spirit among my fellow wrestlers, the mentorship of Prince and the unwavering support of family and friends that sculpted my path.

The opportunity Prince gave me that night remains etched in my heart with everlasting gratitude. His belief in my abilities provided me with a chance to learn and grow as a wrestler, a chance that set the stage for an incredible journey beyond my wildest dreams.

The night was electric, with Texas Hideaway pulsating with the energy of hundreds of enthusiastic attendees. Yet, amid the roaring cheers and the vibrant atmosphere, there were certain individuals whose presence held a special significance for me. Among the sea of faces, it was the familiar countenances of my high school friends—Edwin, Jeremy, Zach and Travis—that stood out. These were the companions who had journeyed with me through the ups and downs of life, who knew the essence of my aspirations, and who now stood by my side as I ventured into the wrestling ring.

It was a testament to the enduring power of friendship that they were there, witnessing a dream I had meticulously worked towards. In those moments, their cheers weren't just noise; they were the embodiment of unwavering support and shared memories. We had laughed, studied and grown up together, and now they were here to share in this pivotal chapter of my life.

But that night's audience wasn't complete without the presence of familiar faces from my past. Among those who had cheered alongside me at the TWA events, some had made their way to this pivotal match. The bonds formed during those formative days of standing in line and sharing our excitement for wrestling had persevered, transcending time and space to converge at this remarkable juncture.

However, as I reflect on that unforgettable night, what truly warms my heart is the memory of my family's presence. There they were, my brother, sister, and parents, occupying seats that held more significance than any championship belt. Their support wasn't merely a gesture; it was a testament to the unbreakable connection that binds families together. Their presence represented countless rides to practices, hours spent watching wrestling matches on television, and the steady stream of encouragement that had fueled my journey.

Me and my older brother Adrian.

In a world often marked by chaos and uncertainty, it's the unwavering support of loved ones that anchors us. The resonance of their cheers that night wasn't confined to the arena; it echoed in my heart, a reminder that the pursuit of dreams isn't a solitary endeavor. Their belief in me fortified my determination, and their presence transformed that match into a shared experience—a celebration of resilience, hard work and the bonds that transcend bloodlines.

My brother Adrian, my very first tag team partner in life, holds a special place in my heart as one of my most ardent supporters. Through the twists and turns of life, he's been a steadfast presence in my corner, cheering me on with unwavering pride. His belief in me has always been a source of strength, a reminder that our bond extends beyond the wrestling ring.

Equally instrumental in my journey has been my sister Lauren, a pillar of unwavering support who has stood by me through thick and thin. Her encouragement has been a driving force, propelling me forward even in moments of doubt. Her presence in the crowd, her voice joining the chorus of cheers, has lent me the strength to push through challenges and embrace triumphs.

The dynamic with my mother has its own unique color, as she's taken on the role of my most vocal defender. In her eyes, the world of wrestling is still very real, and her maternal instincts kick into high gear when she sees fans booing against me. She's shown me that her love is as fierce as it is protective, and I've marveled at her ability to fearlessly engage in friendly battles with those who dare to jeer. Her unshakable belief in me, even when the lines between fiction and reality blur, has been both endearing and inspiring.

To my Mom, I want to convey my deep appreciation and gratitude. Your unwavering support, boundless love, and unyielding dedication have been the cornerstone of my journey in the wrestling world. From the earliest days of my wrestling aspirations to the countless matches I've competed in, your presence has been a guiding light.

The memory of your cheers from the stands, your encouraging words before matches, and your fierce defense of me against any naysayers resonate deeply within me. You've stood by me through the highs and lows of this unpredictable path, offering both a source of strength and a reminder of the unwavering love of family.

Like a true champion, you've stepped into the ring of life with courage and determination, setting an example that I strive to emulate in my own endeavors. As I've wrestled to achieve my goals, your belief in me has served as a powerful motivator, propelling me forward when faced with challenges. Just as you've championed me, I want you to know that you are a true champion in my eyes. Your sacrifices, your patience, and your boundless support have shaped me into the person I am today. With every match, every triumph, and every lesson learned, I carry your spirit with me.

My father has become an integral part of my wrestling journey, a steadfast presence who is welcomed and respected wherever I step into the ring. Wrestlers extend to him the utmost respect, embracing him as a member of their extended family. This bond, forged through shared experiences and mutual admiration, carries a profound significance.

It's a touching realization that my father, the man who dedicated countless hours to driving me to training and supporting my dreams, was there to witness my inaugural match. Over two decades later, his commitment remains steadfast as he continues to attend the majority of my matches. While I understand that the passage of time inevitably brings change, for now, I am grateful for the moments we've shared.

My father and I with the AWR Sean Patrick's Title in 2023. He's my hero and my biggest supporter.

As of this writing, my father is 84 years old, a remarkable individual who embodies strength, resilience, and a tireless work ethic. A Vietnam veteran and a two-time retiree, his life story is a testament to his enduring spirit. He's a man who leads with his heart, demonstrating the qualities I aspire to emulate as a future father. Every day, he inspires me to be a better version of myself, and I hope he recognizes how deeply his influence shapes my path.

To my Dad, I express my heartfelt gratitude. Every sacrifice, every moment of support, and every silent encouragement have left an indelible mark on my life. The memory of his presence at that pivotal first match and his continued presence in my journey are cherished beyond words. As I continue to wrestle and pursue my passions, I carry with me the lessons he's imparted and the love he's shown. Thank you, Dad, for being there to share in a moment that will forever remain etched in my memory.

With every step I take, lacing up my boots and stepping into the ring, I carry the invaluable lessons learned from that night. Wrestling has shown me that success isn't solely measured by championships and accolades; it's about the impact we have on the lives of others. It's about inspiring the next generation of wrestlers and connecting with fans in a profound and meaningful way.

The wrestling business is notorious for its harsh reality - it doesn't owe anyone anything. This sentiment was particularly evident when I was just 16 years old and eager to step into the world of professional wrestling. At that age, the business had nothing to give me, not even the simple gesture of allowing me to train.

As a young and passionate individual, I was ready to take on the world, or in this case, the wrestling ring. But the reality was far from the dreams that fueled my enthusiasm. The wrestling business is a tough and unforgiving industry, and age and passion alone weren't enough to gain entry.

Many promotions and schools have strict age restrictions, and rightfully so. The physical demands and risks involved in professional wrestling require a level of maturity and responsibility that often comes with age and experience. So, at 16, I found myself facing closed door after closed door until Prince and ACW opened one for me and allowed my dream to come true the night of March 3rd, 2001.

For every aspiring wrestling trainee, the day of their first match is a momentous occasion. It's a dream that flickers in the back of your mind, and traditionally, you never really know when it's going to happen. I've witnessed countless individuals in this business suddenly thrust into their debut matches, seemingly out of nowhere.

In the world of wrestling, opportunities can arise unexpectedly. You might be working backstage as a security guard, announcer, music guy, or even a referee, and then the booker comes up to you with that magical question, "Do you have your wrestling gear?" It's an unspoken rule to have your gear ready at all times because you never know when you might be added to the card.

I consider myself fortunate because I had a rare privilege - the luxury of knowing well over a month in advance that my first match was on the horizon. I had plenty of preparation time, and I recognized the value of such a precious opportunity. However, it also came with a sense of responsibility, as I hadn't earned this chance in the traditional sense. With just three months of training under my belt, I was still learning the fundamentals of wrestling, barely grasping how to take a bump correctly. Yet, there I was, with the remarkable opportunity to step into the ring and showcase my skills. The weight of this privilege was not lost on me.

As I look back on my wrestling journey, I can't help but smile at the flood of memories that wash over me. The resounding applause of the crowd, the enthusiasm backstage shared with fellow wrestlers, the surge of adrenaline coursing through my veins before entering the ring – all of these experiences have shaped me not only as a wrestler but also as a person.

Through every twist and turn, I've remained humbled by the unwavering support of the wrestling community. The fans who cheer me on, the fellow wrestlers who challenge and inspire me, and the mentors who have selflessly guided my path – they have all played a profound role in my growth as a wrestler and as a human being.

Standing here, years after that first match, I am filled with immense gratitude for every step of this incredible journey. Wrestling has given me more than I ever dared to dream. It has taught me the true essence of perseverance, dedication, and the courage to pursue one's dreams without fear.

No matter the number of matches I've performed in or the accolades I've earned, that debut at the 1-year anniversary show will forever hold a special place in my heart. It was the spark that ignited a relentless fire within me, driving me to push the boundaries of what I believed was possible.

As time has passed, my journey in the wrestling world has brought me to a unique and fulfilling role - being part of several people's first matches. It's a humbling experience to stand on the other end of the spectrum, looking into the nervous and anxious faces of these newcomers, just as I once stood on that precipice.

Love being the first match of new wrestlers.

As I watch them prepare for their debut, I can't help but see a reflection of my younger self in their eyes. The mix of excitement and fear is often noticeable in all of their eyes, and it takes me back to the early days of my own wrestling career. In those moments, I am reminded of the invaluable support and guidance I received from those who came before me, and I am determined to pay it forward.

It's an honor beyond words to be part of these newcomers' first steps in the wrestling ring, especially when it involves one of my own students. As a teacher and mentor, I've watched them grow and develop, and now, standing by their side during their debut match, I feel a sense of pride like no other.

In these matches, I am more than just an opponent; I am a mentor, a supporter, and a cheerleader for their success. The dynamic is different from my own first match, where nerves and inexperience led to a brief encounter. Now, I am there to guide them through the experience, offering encouragement and reassurance that they are capable of shining in the ring.

As the bell rings, and the match begins, I am filled with a mix of emotions - excitement for their journey ahead and a desire to create a memorable experience for them. It's my chance to let them shine, to showcase their talents and abilities, and to help them make their mark in the wrestling world. And just for clarification, these matches are way longer than a minute and 42 seconds and I often let them win.

These matches are not just about the physical battle in the ring; they represent a passing of the torch, a connection between generations of wrestlers. And when the match concludes, it's a privilege to see the joy and satisfaction on their faces, just as I once felt after my own debut.

As I continue to be part of these memorable moments, I am reminded of the cyclical nature of wrestling. The support and guidance I received in my early days have now become my responsibility to offer to the next generation of wrestlers. It's a responsibility I hold dear, knowing that I have the power to positively impact someone's wrestling journey. I know that just as I once stood in their shoes, they too will carry this experience with them, and someday, they may find themselves in my position, paying it forward to the next wave of aspiring wrestlers.

As I continue to lace up my boots and step into the ring, I am grateful for every opportunity to entertain, inspire, and leave a lasting impact. Wrestling has taught me that, no matter where life's journey takes me, the true destination lies in the hearts of those I touch along the way. And for that, I am eternally and humbly thankful.

Chapter 4
Navigating Wrestling's 'He Said, She Said Bullshit'

As I continued to step into the ring at ACW, I encountered an array of experiences that shaped my wrestling journey. While some matches were filled with excitement and triumph, others were far from being classics. In fact, the majority of my matches were meticulously planned, spot for spot, leaving little room for improvisation. Although it allowed for some visually impressive sequences, this style of wrestling eventually presented a challenge when I ventured out on my own years later.

Being reliant on pre-planned spots hindered my ability to call a match on the fly, limiting my creativity and adaptability in the ring. It became apparent that I needed to develop a more versatile approach to wrestling if I wanted to grow and thrive as a performer. This realization led me to seek guidance from someone who had not only mastered the technical aspects of wrestling but also possessed the ability to think on their feet during a match.

Enter Tom Jones, also known as The UK Kid, a pivotal figure in my development as a wrestler. His mentorship was crucial during these times, providing me with the much-needed guidance to overcome the challenges I faced. His experience as a technical stud and his talent for calling matches on the fly became invaluable lessons for me. Under his watchful eye, I learned the art of storytelling in the ring, seamlessly transitioning from move to move while keeping the audience engaged.

The UK Kid became more than just a mentor; he was a guiding force that empowered me to explore my creativity and embrace the spontaneity of wrestling. With his guidance, I gradually shed the shackles of over-planning, allowing myself to adapt to the ebb and flow of each match organically. This transformation not only improved my in-ring performances but also rekindled my passion for wrestling as an art form.

Embracing the lessons learned from The UK Kid, I began to incorporate a blend of technical prowess and improvisation into my matches. This newfound approach allowed me to connect with the audience on a deeper level, making each match a unique and engaging experience for everyone involved. I discovered that the magic of wrestling lies not only in executing impressive moves but also in telling a compelling story that captivates the hearts and minds of the fans.

Me and UK Kid were not only close in age but also in heart, and that connection played a pivotal role in forging a strong bond between us. Among the guys at ACW, he stood out as the most relatable and friendly, yet he had a sternness that commanded respect. His coaching style was nothing short of brilliant, often leading to those "aha" moments that opened our eyes to the true essence of the wrestling business.

Beyond his coaching prowess, UK Kid's sense of humor was infectious. I'll admit, when I first met someone from the United Kingdom, I couldn't help but poke fun at his accent, especially when he pronounced "H's" in his own unique way. The banter and camaraderie we shared further strengthened our friendship and made every training session a joyous adventure.

UK Kid became my first wrestling mentor, and his influence on my early wrestling days was immeasurable. Being a graduate of the revered Shawn Michaels Wrestling Academy only added to the weight of his expertise. Under his guidance, I not only improved my in-ring skills but also gained a deeper understanding of the inner workings and traditions of the wrestling world.

During my time at ACW, I swiftly found myself immersed in my first wrestling angle. The creative team had concocted a concept that slotted me into a stable known as "Heavy Artillery." My tag team partner and I assumed roles akin to the comedic duo of The Three Stooges within the wrestling world. Our gig was to engage in sneaky skirmishes behind the backs of our stablemates, Eurocane and Tank. We would bicker and pretend to be at odds, only to flip the switch and appear entirely innocent whenever they turned their attention our way. The humor and antics that ensued were genuinely entertaining, adding a comedic flavor to the mix.

However, this lighthearted dynamic eventually led us down a path of rivalry. Eurocane, one of our stablemates, challenged us to a "loser leaves the stable" match on August 18th, 2001. It was a captivating twist in the story line, marking my first experience with a story line-driven conflict within a wrestling promotion.

I found myself on the losing end of the "loser leaves the stable" match. As a result, I embarked on a brief stint as a singles wrestler. However, my wrestling journey took a fresh turn when an exciting opportunity presented itself – teaming up with my high school friend Zach to form a tag team partnership.

Super rare photo of Zach as "Cowboy" Shane Cody

Although our tag team experience was in its infancy with only one match under our belt, the thrill of sharing the ring with a close friend brought an extra layer of excitement to the wrestling experience. Zach's persona as "Cowboy Shane Cody" added a unique flavor to our team. His cowboy gimmick, complete with the hat and all, was a standout in the ring and resonated with audiences.

Notably, Zach's charisma and wrestling skills caught the attention of promoters beyond our local scene. He was offered an opportunity to wrestle elsewhere, including with UK Kid. This achievement was a testament to his dedication and talent, and I couldn't help but feel an immense sense of pride for his accomplishments. Throughout it all, watching Zach's growth and success in wrestling was both rewarding and inspiring.

I've got a pretty wild tale to share about the time my ACW buddies and I headed to another local promotion to catch Zach and UK Kid in action. Tank, who was right beside me in the front row, joined us for the wrestling showdown. The night took an unexpected turn when a fellow wrestler emerged and directed a stream of water right at us. Tank's expression of disbelief and bewilderment was quite the spectacle.

But the story doesn't end there. Instead of leaving it at a mere splash, the wrestler continued his watery antics, showering us once more. We were left wondering if this was intentional, perhaps a cheeky interaction knowing who we were, or simply an amusing coincidence.

However, the real twist came as the actual wrestling commenced. The provocation proved too much for Tank's patience. With a steel chair in hand, he leaped into the ring, ready to take matters into his own hands. The wrestler who had doused us with water found himself on the receiving end of Tank's wrath, as he unleashed a flurry of attacks that sent shock waves through the audience.

I was completely speechless and utterly stunned by the unfolding chaos. Almost instantaneously, a surge of wrestlers emerged from the backstage area, storming toward the ring. Amid the frenzy, UK Kid managed to join the tumultuous fray, mixing it up with even more grapplers. Not to be outdone, a couple of my ACW pals threw themselves into the mix, adding their brawling energy to the already frenetic scene.

As the ring became a whirlwind of action and wrestlers clashed in an impromptu melee, I confess I stepped aside, a blend of shock and bewilderment washing over me. In those moments, the mix of emotions, the rapid escalation, and the sheer unpredictability of it all left me momentarily at a loss. It was an instance where the boundary between the scripted world and the genuine passion and intensity of the wrestling community blurred.

I wish I could regale you with a tale of how I courageously leaped into the chaos, throwing punches and contributing to the fray, but the reality is quite different. Instead of joining the wild locker room brawl that was unfolding in front of the crowd, I found myself stepping in between some of the guys, aiming to defuse the situation. There were no dramatic wrestling moves or heroic actions on my part.

Truth be told, the whole incident turned out to be quite embarrassing for Zach, UK Kid and me. Looking back, however, there's an ironic amusement to the situation. While we didn't exactly become the center of attention in a wild ring skirmish, the memory has transformed into a lighthearted and amusing memory.

Now, let's dive into that tag match that Zach and I ventured into. The match was on February 16th, 2002. We decided to embrace a cowboy gimmick, and

I even donned a matching vest to complement his look. Our opponents for the match were none other than Shell Shock, who was actually the son of one of my father's longtime friends, and my former Heavy Artillery tag partner was his teammate. This wasn't just another bout; it felt like wrestling within an extended family circle.

The match itself exuded an old-school vibe, with double-team maneuvers taking center stage. Zach and I unleashed an array of tactics, ranging from a unique drop-down bulldog to synchronized clotheslines and a medley of other maneuvers we hadn't previously explored. Looking back, it was perhaps the most technically intricate tag team match we had engaged in at that point.

The energy of the crowd that night was palpable, and it seemed like the fans were getting behind our tag team efforts. The crowd's enthusiasm further fueled our performance, pushing us to deliver our best in the ring.

As fate would have it, shortly after this memorable tag match, Zach's wrestling journey took an unexpected turn. Life's demands and commitments crept in, causing him to step away from both wrestling and training. Nevertheless, our friendship has endured the test of time, and to this day, we find ourselves reminiscing about the days we spent together in ACW.

As my wrestling journey continued at ACW, an unexpected opportunity arose when The UK Kid extended an invitation to wrestle for Pro Wrestling International (PWI), a promotion with a rich history. PWI held a special place in my heart, being the very foundation from which Shawn Michaels grew his wrestling school and promotion, eventually becoming the renowned Texas Wrestling Alliance (TWA).

Meeting the promoter of PWI, Roland, was a turning point in my wrestling journey. Little did I know that this encounter would mark the beginning of a long-term friendship that continues to thrive to this day. As I shook his hand, I couldn't help but feel a sense of gratitude for the opportunity he presented—to wrestle my mentor UK Kid on November 25th, 2001.

PWI had a slightly go-as-you-please approach compared to what I was used to, but I knew that to truly thrive in the wrestling business, I would have to learn how to adapt and navigate any situation that came my way. It was a sink-or-swim moment, and I was determined to give it my all and rise to the challenge.

I owe a debt of gratitude to Roland for even giving me the time of day and providing me with my first match outside of my home promotion. His belief in me and willingness to offer opportunities played a significant role in my growth as a wrestler.

The prospect of wrestling at PWI filled me with excitement and nerves. At the time, I had less than 10 matches under my belt, and the idea of going out to experience a real match with a trained wrestler was intimidating and exhilarating. The venue's outdoor patio, nestled within a bar and car wash, exuded a raw charm that set the stage for a memorable experience. The atmosphere was electric, with local wrestling fans fueling the anticipation, some enjoying a few beers before the show. It was a stark departure from ACW's familiar setting, but the genuine passion and energy of the crowd invigorated me.

Stepping into the ring with The UK Kid was a dream come true. He was not only a talented wrestler but also a mentor I looked up to with deep admiration. Our match proved to be a profound learning experience, as I encountered moves I had never experienced before, like his signature super kick. The chemistry we shared in the ring was undeniable, and the thrill of the moment left an indelible mark on my wrestling journey.

Over 20 years have passed since that unforgettable match with UK Kid, and to this day, it remains one of my top 10 favorites with a deeply sentimental meaning. It was a pivotal moment in my wrestling journey, as UK Kid pushed me beyond my limits, challenging me to showcase advanced wrestling spots that I had never attempted before in a match.

As the adrenaline surged through my veins, I found myself executing moves like a top rope crossbody, a spinning head scissors, a tornado DDT, and a sunset flip in the corner—maneuvers that I once thought were beyond my reach. It was a moment of revelation, realizing the vast potential I had within me and the heights I could achieve with the right guidance and determination.

The memories of that match are etched in my mind, as clear as if it happened yesterday. It was a defining moment in my wrestling career, one that transformed my perspective on the sport and bolstered my confidence as a performer.

But beyond the technical prowess and the exhilarating moves, that match held a deeper significance for me. It was a testament to the friendship and mentorship I shared with the UK Kid. His belief in my abilities and his support paved the way for my growth as a wrestler.

Me vs. UK Kid at PWI

In the years that followed, I would carry a piece of UK Kid with me into every match, as I adopted some of his catchphrases and signature moves. Whenever you hear me shout, "Who sucks now?" to the crowd while executing a headlock, it is a homage to the UK Kid, a tribute to the impact he had on my career.

Following the show, my first-ever payment for wrestling was handed to me - a modest sum of $5. While it may have seemed insignificant as wrestling pay, the experience was priceless. It symbolized a milestone - my first taste of recognition as a wrestler and the validation of my dedication to the sport.

The experience at PWI broadened my horizons in the world of independent wrestling. It introduced me to a diverse range of wrestlers, from seasoned veterans to fellow newcomers like myself. The encounter also highlighted the vastness of knowledge and experience I had yet to gain in the indy wrestling scene.

The UK Kid's mentorship proved to be instrumental in my development as a wrestler, especially as I ventured beyond the safe confines of ACW. His guidance and support became more crucial than ever as I navigated the unpredictable waters of the wrestling scene. With The UK Kid's insight and teachings, I felt more equipped to handle the challenges that lay ahead.

From that point forward, my wrestling journey took an interesting turn as I was extended an invitation to perform on multiple PWI shows. The prospect of working in different promotions brought a mix of excitement and confusion. While I was eager to explore new opportunities, I couldn't help but feel a sense of loyalty to Prince and ACW, the place where my wrestling dreams had begun.

As a 16-year-old kid, I lacked a deep understanding of the intricate workings of the wrestling business. Prince's reaction to my decision to work in another promotion highlighted his protective nature towards his homegrown talent and students. Prince didn't want us to risk facing unprotected matches against dangerous wrestlers. At the time, I didn't quite see it that way; I perceived it as more of a limitation on our progress. Looking back, I can now comprehend his perspective - he wanted to ensure that his students were well-prepared and safe in their wrestling endeavors.

Being caught between my loyalty to Prince and my gratitude to The UK Kid, who had been crucial in my development as a wrestler, put me in a challenging position. My next few matches at PWI proved to be significant learning experiences. I found myself grappling with local, seasoned veterans whose wrestling style was vastly different from what I was accustomed to at ACW.

At ACW, I had been taught to follow a structured and "paint-by-numbers" approach to matches. In contrast, these PWI veterans preferred calling their matches in the ring, without detailed pre-planning. This was a completely foreign concept to me, and I often felt lost like a deer caught in headlights. However, as discouraging as it seemed, this unfamiliar territory turned out to be exactly what I needed to grow as a wrestler.

Wrestling alongside San Antonio veterans who had been in the industry for decades was both awe-inspiring and humbling. Among them were esteemed wrestlers like Rob Summers and Kid Soulja, graduates of the prestigious Shawn Michaels Wrestling Academy. The opportunity to share the ring with such accomplished individuals was a dream come true and a testament to the progress I was making in my wrestling journey.

Looking back, it's a bit embarrassing to reflect on my early days as a 16-year-old kid with limited knowledge in the ring. I couldn't help but wonder if the audience or the more experienced roster could see the nervousness and uncertainty I felt. But thankfully, every wrestler I had the privilege of wrestling with at PWI took care of me, offering support and guidance.

Embracing the challenge of stepping into the ring unprepared, without a script to follow, pushed me to think on my feet and adapt to unpredictable situations. It was a crucial lesson in the art of improvisation and trusting my instincts as a performer. Though I encountered some missteps along the way, these experiences ultimately taught me to be more versatile and adaptable in the wrestling world.

Despite my enthusiasm and belief in my abilities, Prince's concerns were not entirely unfounded. Our disagreements over my involvement with PWI led to heated discussions. In hindsight, I recognize that I should have approached the situation with more understanding and respect for Prince's perspective. Nevertheless, the friction between us ultimately fueled my determination to prove myself and demonstrate my readiness for whatever the wrestling world had in store.

One evening, we gathered at Prince's house for a meeting, and the topic of ACW students exploring opportunities to wrestle elsewhere was brought up. I distinctly recall feeling a surge of emotion when Prince expressed his concern about this. To me, it seemed like he was questioning the confidence that UK Kid, one of the trainers, had in us as students. He also had a few words to say about Spiro and Slayer.

What made it particularly upsetting was that UK Kid, Spiro and Slayer weren't present during the meeting, so they couldn't defend themselves or share their perspective on the matter. It felt unfair that Prince raised his concerns without giving any of the guys training us the chance to be part of the conversation.

As a student under UK Kid's mentorship, I had come to greatly admire him. His coaching had been invaluable to my growth as a wrestler, and his belief in us as individuals meant the world. So when Prince's comments seemed to undermine that trust and confidence, it struck a nerve.

I understood that Prince might have had genuine concerns about us exploring other opportunities, but I believed that UK Kid's guidance and support should be enough to assure him of our dedication and commitment to ACW. It was a testament to the strong bond we had with UK Kid, and it was disappointing to see that not everyone shared that same level of faith in us.

At that moment, I felt the need to speak up and protect UK Kid's reputation and the trust he had given us. What I really wanted was for Prince to understand that just because we had been working elsewhere, it didn't mean our loyalty was divided. I wanted to reassure him that our dedication to ACW was still strong.

As the meeting unfolded, I made my feelings known, expressing my offense at the suggestion that we might be disloyal or uncommitted. I shared my gratitude for UK Kid's mentorship and made it clear that exploring other opportunities didn't mean we were turning our backs on ACW. Instead, it was a chance for us to grow and learn, carrying the lessons and passion instilled in us by UK Kid.

After that eventful introduction to PWI, I continued wrestling for ACW for about three more months. Unfortunately, the strain caused by my branching out to other promotions created a toxic environment. My decision to explore new opportunities created tension in my relationship with Prince, and I regretted that our once-strong bond had faltered. Nevertheless, I remained grateful for the invaluable foundation and support that ACW had provided during my year of training and wrestling with them.

I remember right after that meeting, I wasted no time in reaching out to UK Kid to share all the details that were discussed. Something about the whole situation just didn't sit right with me. It felt wrong that there were conversations happening behind people's backs, especially targeting individuals like UK Kid, Spiro, and Slayer.

In hindsight, maybe I should have stayed out of it. After all, the matters being discussed were clearly above my pay grade. But I couldn't shake off the feeling that something needed to be said, that the truth needed to be brought to light. Little did I know that my involvement would come back to haunt me. I was about to receive a stark introduction to the harsh realities of the wrestling business, a glimpse into what can happen when someone within the promotion wants to push you out.

My final ACW show on March 23rd, 2002 took a wild turn I never saw coming. After what was supposed to be a quick loss in my match, I ended up in an unexpected and brutally eye-opening situation. There I was, lying in the ring, trying to catch my breath after getting pinned, when I noticed Spiro and Slayer making their way toward me. What came next was completely out of left field. They unleashed a barrage of forearms, chops, and even pulled off an impromptu double spine buster on me. None of this was anywhere in the script. After the chaos, I distinctly heard Slayer's voice cutting through, saying, "Hey kid, steer clear of all that he said, she said crap."

It hit me like a ton of bricks. Their unexpected attack was meant to send a message, a very physical one at that. It was a lesson, ordered by Prince, a "shoot" in wrestling terms, and it wasn't scripted. But I could tell they were holding back a bit, not giving me the full force of what they were capable of. I found out later, it was because UK Kid asked them to not hurt me.

Backstage, changing out of my wrestling gear, the whole situation sank in. It was a clear sign that my time with ACW was over. It was a stark reminder that the wrestling world was more than just the action inside the ring. Behind the scenes, there were politics, unwritten rules and moments like these meant to establish authority.

As March of 2002 rolled around, I made the difficult but necessary decision to move forward and seek training elsewhere. While my time at ACW had come to an end, the experiences I gained there served as building blocks for the wrestling journey that lay ahead.

As I continued my journey in the wrestling business, I soon learned that the relationships within this world can be as unpredictable as the matches themselves. Friends and associates came and went, and I experienced the ever-shifting dynamics of this close-knit community. Sometimes, you could form strong bonds with fellow wrestlers or promoters, only to find yourself at odds with them over something seemingly trivial or, at times, something intensely dramatic. It was a side of wrestling I had never known existed, and it opened my eyes to the politics and etiquette that governed the industry.

During my early days, I was not fully aware of the intricacies and unspoken rules that govern the wrestling world. Naively, I assumed that talent alone would be enough to sustain relationships and keep everyone united. However, as I ventured out to explore different promotions and opportunities, I quickly realized that loyalty and trust played significant roles in this interconnected world.

My decision to pursue opportunities outside of ACW strained my relationship with Prince Fontenot and the guys at ACW. It was a tough lesson to learn, but it highlighted the importance of respecting the bonds that had been formed within the promotion. I regretted not being able to patch things up at the time, but I was grateful that the passage of time eventually led to the mending of those strained relationships.

As I matured in the wrestling business, I began to understand the delicate balance of navigating both personal and professional relationships. I learned that mutual respect and communication were vital in maintaining positive connections within the wrestling community. While disagreements and conflicts were inevitable, approaching them with humility and understanding often paved the way for resolution.

Looking back on those early days, I see how crucial it was for me to experience these challenges and obstacles. It shaped me as a person and as a wrestler, teaching me the value of both loyalty and independence. It was a valuable lesson in appreciating the support of those who shared the same passion for wrestling, while also embracing the courage to venture into uncharted territory and forge my path in the industry.

In the end, I realized that the wrestling business is a tight-knit family, and every member contributes to its unique fabric. Though the road may be filled with unexpected twists and turns, I emerged from those experiences with a greater understanding of the intricacies that underlie this thrilling and unpredictable world of professional wrestling.

One prevailing truth about the wrestling business is its cynicism—the idea that you'll encounter familiar faces both on your way up and on your way down. People come and go, and the wrestling journey is riddled with twists and turns. Amidst this complexity, one golden rule stands out: stay true to yourself and avoid engaging in gossip or speaking ill of others. In the wrestling world, bridges are everything. Burning a bridge can have long-lasting consequences, potentially closing doors that could have led to new opportunities. I learned this lesson the hard way during this whole situation when I left ACW.

At the time, I found myself caught up in the "he said, she said" drama. I had good intentions, sticking up for someone I considered a mentor. But as I got entangled in the rumors and hearsay, I lost sight of the bigger picture—the impact my actions might have on my reputation and relationships within the wrestling community at such an early stage in my journey.

Chapter 5
Back to Square One:
Relearning in the Wrestling World

I found myself venturing into new territory by training at PWI during the summer of 2002. The training location was different but full of character - the back of a local wrestler named Tommy Gunn's house, where a 20 x 20 wrestling ring stood, albeit not in the best shape. It was here that I was introduced to "Mad Dog" Ken Johnson, my new trainer.

Ken had a more old-school approach to training, emphasizing the ground and pound techniques and the shoot style of wrestling. He lived up to his "mad dog" gimmick with his wild and party-animal persona. Training with Ken was intense and exhilarating, and it kept me deeply immersed in the PWI circle.

Practicing in a worn-down ring in the backyard might not have been glamorous, but it was where we honed our wrestling craft under Ken's guidance. Travis even joined training with me and Jeremy surprisingly participated for a little bit as well. Despite the less than perfect setting, I am immensely grateful for everything Ken imparted and the opportunities he provided me with. His positive and unwavering support in developing my skills as a pro wrestler were invaluable.

Ken Johnson's presence in the Texas wrestling scene was no small feat; he was a local fixture who had made his mark over the years beginning in 1979. His legacy extended beyond the backyard ring, as he had also wrestled in the illustrious Southwest Championship Wrestling promotion under the guidance of Joe Blanchard. He was also an enhancement talent for the WWE in the 80s. I had the privilege of viewing videos and photos of some of his old school matches against some of the biggest names to grace the Lone Star State, leaving a lasting impression on me.

What made Ken even more remarkable was his connection to the legendary Shawn Michaels Wrestling

Academy, where he once served as a trainer. To be able to learn from someone who had been a part of such esteemed institutions was truly an honor, even if my time under his learning tree was relatively brief.

His dedication to teaching and his belief in my potential were evident in every session. Despite the rough edges, he remained a mentor who pushed me to be my best, even if his approach was a bit maverick at times. Underneath Ken's guidance, I not only developed my in-ring skills but also gained a deeper understanding of the history and essence of Texas wrestling. It was an experience that fueled my passion for the sport and instilled in me a sense of respect for the pioneers who had come before us.

I carry the honor of having been part of his tutelage with pride, as his legacy lives on in every match I step into, a testament to the enduring impact of the Texas wrestling scene and the mentors who shaped its future generations. Wrestling isn't always about the glitz and glamour—it's about the passion and determination that drives us to excel, no matter the setting or circumstances.

So, with gratitude and a touch of nostalgia, I look back on those moments with Ken, remembering the positive impact he had on my journey as a professional wrestler. His belief in my potential and the experience of training under his guidance remain an integral part of my growth in the world of pro wrestling. The lessons I gained from those backyard sessions with Ken are priceless. Wrestling is not always glamorous; it demands perseverance and resilience, both physically and mentally. And while Ken's penchant for a few extra Coors Lights might have added some unpredictability to the mix, it also taught me to adapt and remain focused in any circumstance.

Ken Johnson, though no longer with us, holds a significant place in my wrestling journey. This chapter of my career was deeply intertwined with his contributions, albeit regrettably brief due to my decision to move forward. His presence remains an unerasable memory, marking a pivotal period in my wrestling trajectory.

In early 2002, I ventured into other wrestling companies across the Dallas-Fort Worth region, in what were my first out of town wrestling matches. What's more, Travis and I resumed our wrestling journey together, forming an inseparable wrestling duo for a significant stretch. I recall a particular instance when both Travis and I participated in a wrestling event on

July 26th, 2002, hosted at a local flea market in the Dallas-Fort Worth area for a promotion called American Lone star Lethal Wrestling (ALLW). That night, we engaged in an intense 20-minute match, which not only marked my debut in that area but also introduced me to an entirely new roster of local talents.

My first win was against Travis (Manhattan) almost 2 years into my career.

This match held a special place in my wrestling journey as it marked my very first victory in the ring—an achievement that brought a surge of excitement and pride. What made this bout even more memorable was that it was the sole occasion when I sported my skull mask, a piece of gear I had been eager to incorporate into my persona. The match with Travis unfolded in a classic manner, beginning with a series of chain wrestling and reversals, gradually building up the momentum.

I initiated the action with a headlock followed by a tackle, drop-down maneuver, and then a reverse hip toss. As the pace picked up, I deftly dodged a clothesline and countered with a well-placed elbow and cross body. However, like any wrestling story, the momentum shifted, and my opponent gained the upper hand, subjecting me to his onslaught of offense.

But this was wrestling, and comebacks are a staple of the craft. I persevered, launched into my rally, and finally secured the win with a move that I had envisioned as my potential finishing move at the time —the Unprettier, which was a reverse face buster. It is the same move that Christian Cage in WWE made famous. I always thought it looked cool and I was finally winning so I chose that as my first finishing move. It was a culmination of strategy, skill, and heart, all encapsulated in that victorious moment

The taste of victory was a long time coming, and when it finally arrived, it brought a rush of emotions that I'll never forget. Admittedly, the win was scripted between my friend and me, but it symbolized so much more than just a check mark in the win column. My brother and my dad, who had been steadfast supporters throughout my wrestling journey, were visibly thrilled as they enthusiastically cheered me on from the sidelines. In fact, if you were to watch the tape of that match, you'd catch my brother's exuberant cheers ringing out loudly, a testament to how much this victory meant to us.

Reflecting on it now, the road to that triumph spanned nearly two years, a journey marked by learning curves, challenges, and persistent dedication. Despite the scripted nature of the outcome, that win resonated deeply, not just as a victory but as a representation of progress, growth, and the culmination of countless hours of hard work.

Regrettably, Travis seemed to have a recurring pattern of disappearing from the wrestling scene, a trend that was becoming all too familiar. It was as if he had a gift for entering the wrestling world, only to eventually fade into the shadows without fully committing. This peculiar behavior left me perplexed, as he repeatedly managed to open doors for himself within the business, only to then abruptly withdraw.

In contrast, my aspirations and dedication to the wrestling industry burned even brighter. While Travis grappled with consistency, I had a plethora of dreams waiting to be realized within this dynamic realm. The allure of the ring, the thrill of the crowd's cheers, and the constant drive to better myself in the squared circle kept me resolutely anchored to the path I had chosen.

Me and Travis wrestling in one of our few encounters

This phase of my wrestling journey was undeniably a period of growing pains. Following my departure from the familiar nest of ACW, my life in the wrestling world took on a nomadic quality. Everywhere I turned, I encountered fresh faces, formed new connections, and experienced the ebb and flow of evolving friendships. However, this dynamic landscape came with its share of challenges.

As I ventured into various promotions, I soon realized that the wrestling industry's loyalty was fickle at best. Just as quickly as I'd find my footing within a new promotion, the rug could be pulled out from under me without warning. It was an environment of constant movement, akin to navigating through a maze with no fixed destination. The nature of the indy wrestling scene became increasingly evident: it was a world where your value was often measured in the immediate contributions you could offer, rather than any sustained commitment.

This harsh reality taught me an invaluable lesson: in the indy wrestling circuit, no one owes you anything. It was a place where opportunities could arise overnight and evaporate just as swiftly. I began to understand that I needed to be adaptable, to embrace change, and to be prepared for the unexpected. Each promotion's approach to talent management was unique, and this era of my career was a crucible that tested my resilience and adaptability like never before.

This phase marked a crucial period of growth and a stark realization of how unprepared I was for the world of wrestling. I had a stint in Corsicana, Texas, wrestling for All-Star Pro Wrestling (ASPW), where I was slated to face off against an opponent named the Enigma. As we went over our match details backstage, it seemed like we had everything properly outlined and ready to execute. However, once we stepped into the ring, things immediately took an unexpected turn. The Enigma decided to go off-script and do his own thing, contradicting what we had discussed earlier.

Feeling caught off guard, I tried to adapt to the situation and went along with his improvisations. When it came to executing holds and sequences, I attempted to get the match back on track by calling the first spot. The plan was for him to execute a spinning head scissors after I shot him off. But as I executed the move, he didn't follow through with the spinning head scissors, leaving me in a moment of confusion.

The match quickly devolved into chaos, becoming an embarrassing and frustrating experience. I felt the need to salvage what was left of the situation and suggested that we wrap it up and conclude the match in less than five minutes. I couldn't determine whether our lack of experience collectively led to this debacle or if the Enigma simply chose not to cooperate.

Having departed from the safety net of ACW and the guidance of my mentors who meticulously went over matches step by step, I found myself thrust into the unforgiving realm of indy wrestling. Here, the rules were different – not everyone adhered to the structured routines, and not everyone prioritized ensuring that every move was executed as planned. It was a cutthroat environment where one's survival depended on their adaptability and resilience. And in this harsh reality, I was quickly learning the harsh lessons that came with it.

I may have learned a lot during this time, but I felt I could be doing more with my passion about the wrestling business. One thing that I could say about a lot of young kids in wrestling is they tend to do dumb things when they first go out on their own away from the nest of their wrestling school. I was no exception.

During this time, I had an ambitious and wild idea brewing in my mind - starting my own wrestling promotion. The dream of running my own shows, creating story lines, and booking talented wrestlers filled my thoughts. It was a bold and daring vision, and though I was still relatively new to the wrestling scene, the passion and determination were unstoppable.

To show how serious I was about this idea, I shelled out $2000 to buy a professional wrestling ring. Yes, a 17 year old kid went out and bought a ring to try to accomplish the crazy idea of running a wrestling show. I also had the ridiculous idea that I would get my high school friends with HWF to train under me.

I shared my grand idea of starting my own wrestling promotion with my mentor, The UK Kid, he responded with a healthy dose of reality. He didn't sugarcoat his thoughts and instead offered me some candid advice that I needed to hear.

He reminded me that I was only a year into the wrestling business and still just a 17-year-old kid. He cautioned me that the wrestling industry could be brutal and unforgiving, especially for someone new and inexperienced like me. UK Kid emphasized that being taken seriously as a promoter would be an uphill battle, and many people in the business might try to take advantage of my naivety.

I really bought a wrestling ring for a graduation present.

He warned me that running a wrestling promotion involved financial risks and a lot of responsibilities, and if I wasn't careful, I could end up losing a significant amount of money. It was a wake-up call, and I realized that my passion and enthusiasm alone wouldn't be enough to navigate the challenges that awaited me.

UK Kid's honesty and genuine concern for my well-being made me pause and reflect on my decision. While the idea of running my own wrestling promotion was enticing, I had to consider whether I was truly ready for such a venture. I took his advice to heart and acknowledged that I still had much to learn both in and out of the ring.

After expressing my gratitude to The UK Kid for his honest advice, he offered me another valuable suggestion. He recommended that if I were going to invest money in wrestling, I should seriously consider enrolling at the Texas Wrestling Academy under the guidance of Rudy Boy Gonzalez (RBG). Rudy was a respected figure in the wrestling world, having been a wrestler on the Texas Wrestling Alliance shows alongside Shawn Michaels and a trainer at the Shawn Michaels Wrestling Academy.

In the summer of 2002, the Shawn Michaels school shut its doors since Shawn Michaels had gone back to WWE on a full-time basis. This led Rudy to take the opportunity to rename everything as the Texas Wrestling Academy. While I had come across both positive and negative feedback about Rudy from different sources, I hadn't had a chance to meet him face-to-face. Despite this, I carefully considered my choices and reached the decision that this could be the perfect route to advance my wrestling career.

Without hesitation, I reached out to RBG, inquiring whether I could attend his school despite being only 17 years old with just a year of wrestling experience. To my surprise, RBG promptly responded, inviting me to visit the Texas Wrestling Academy the following day.

Stepping into Rudy Boy Gonzalez's wrestling school marked a significant moment in my wrestling journey. The academy, situated down the road from ACW's flea market venue, was housed in a metal building resembling a body shop. As I walked in, my excitement soared when I spotted Brian Kendrick and American Dragon. They had recently been released from WWE developmental deals and were now making waves in Ring of Honor (ROH). I couldn't resist introducing myself and expressing my admiration for their talent.

With enthusiasm, I shared that I was a big fan of theirs and had seen their early matches at TWA. To my delight, Brian Kendrick responded with a self-deprecating smile, "how embarrassing." His lighthearted remark left me chuckling, and I was thrilled by how approachable and friendly they both were. It was a surreal experience to have a casual chat with wrestlers I had looked up to and watched in action during my early wrestling days.

Soon after, Rudy himself appeared, and I took a seat as he inquired about my wrestling background. With 18 matches under my belt, I had some experience, and I eagerly shared my training journey under the guidance of UK Kid, Prince, and Ken Johnson at ACW and PWI. Rudy was forthright, telling me that I would need to start from scratch and get retrained by him. I anticipated this, understanding that I had much to learn before taking on more experienced opponents.

Undeterred, I was determined to invest in my wrestling education. When Rudy mentioned the cost of training, I didn't hesitate; I handed over the payment in cash, ready to embark on this new chapter of my wrestling odyssey. With that transaction, I officially became a student of the Texas Wrestling Academy, an extension of the legacy of Shawn Michaels' school. The fact that Rudy allowed a 17-year-old like me to train spoke volumes about his dedication to nurturing aspiring wrestlers and building a strong wrestling community.

Enrolling at the Texas Wrestling Academy under Rudy Boy Gonzalez's guidance was a dream come true for me. His reputation as a trainer of stars preceded him, and I was well aware of the success stories that had emerged from his school. While nothing was guaranteed in this unpredictable industry, I knew I was stepping into a facility that took wrestling seriously, and that fact alone exhilarated me.

From day one, Rudy wasted no time in putting me through the paces. It was an intense cardio regimen that pushed me to my limits. Despite having some experience under my belt, I had to let go of any preconceived notions and humble myself to start afresh with the basics. The pre-warm-up mat drills, squats, crunches, push-ups, and rigorous running sessions were just the beginning, all before I even had the chance to step into the ring for bumping practice. And let me tell you, the training academy was an absolute sweat city – the heat turned up the intensity to a whole new level.

Officially, training took place five days a week in the evenings after 7 pm, but the unspoken rule was that if you were truly serious about your craft, you had to be there early, around 5 pm, and stay long after the scheduled time. The dedication of my fellow trainees was awe-inspiring, and if you really meant business, you'd even show up on Saturday mornings to train. The doors were always open, and I quickly realized that everyone I met at Rudy's school shared an unwavering commitment to their wrestling journey.

Walking into the Texas Wrestling Academy, I was met with a group of seasoned adults, some of them built like tanks, all fiercely dedicated to perfecting their craft. Each and everyone of these guys meant business and I was out of my league. As the 17-year-old in this group, I felt the weight of responsibility to prove myself and earn my place in this professional and wrestling-focused community.

Rudy "Boy" Gonzalez

Rudy Boy Gonzalez, a notable figure in the wrestling world, was the most decorated mentor I had the privilege of being trained by at that time. From the moment I stepped into his Texas Wrestling Academy, I knew I was in the presence of someone truly exceptional. Rudy's wealth of experience as a wrestler and his reputation for producing successful talent made him an invaluable asset to my wrestling journey.

Throughout his illustrious career, Rudy had experienced the rigors of wrestling firsthand. He broke into the business in 1982, under the banner of Southwest Championship Wrestling in San Antonio, Texas. During those early days, he had the invaluable opportunity to work with a crew of seasoned veterans, including renowned names like Tiger Conway Jr, "Wahoo" McDaniel, Tully Blanchard, Chavo Guerrero, and many others. These wrestling legends played a pivotal role in shaping his journey, and among them, he holds the "Ragin Bull" Manny Fernandez in special regard for being a significant influence.

Under Rudy's guidance, I quickly discovered that he was more than just a trainer; he became a father figure to many of us aspiring wrestlers. His dedication to honing our skills and instilling discipline in the ring was matched only by the genuine care and concern he showed for each of his students. With every lesson, he nurtured not only our wrestling abilities but also our character and professionalism.

One of the most crucial aspects of my time at the Texas Wrestling Academy was learning the art of wrestling psychology. Rudy instilled in us the importance of storytelling within the ring. I quickly picked up the correct way to structure a match, building anticipation and crafting moments that would resonate with the audience. This deeper understanding of wrestling psychology allowed me to connect with the crowd on a whole new level and elevate my performances to new heights.

The training sessions at the academy were intense and rigorous. From the pre-warm-up mat drills to the grueling cardio sessions, we were pushed to our limits. But Rudy's commitment to excellence and his emphasis on starting with a solid foundation made every challenge worthwhile. I found myself immersed in an environment of passionate and dedicated wrestlers who shared the same desire to excel in this craft.

Beyond the wrestling techniques, Rudy also imparted invaluable life lessons that extended far beyond the squared circle. His mentorship taught us the importance of perseverance, respect, and resiliency - traits that would serve us not only in wrestling but in all aspects of life.

Rudy Boy Gonzalez's training style was undoubtedly tough, and he had a no-nonsense approach that might have seemed harsh at times. But, I came to understand that this old-school mentality was rooted in his passion for the wrestling business. In this industry, success requires dedication, hard work, and a willingness to push yourself beyond your limits.

In an era vastly different from today, Rudy and his peers had to earn their place in the wrestling world through hard work, respect, and dedication. The feedback they received was often direct and straightforward, and it was all about striving for excellence. The training environment at Rudy's school was no exception. It was completely no-nonsense during training time, ensuring that every moment was dedicated to honing our skills and preparing us for the challenges of the wrestling world.

From one of my first matches at Rudy Boy's ETW

While it might have been tough at times, I came to appreciate the value of criticism and the wisdom of learning from veterans like Rudy. I understood that this was the way of the wrestling business, and as new guys like me, it was our responsibility to honor and respect that tradition. Despite the occasional hurt feelings, I recognized that this approach was what made the wrestling industry so unique and compelling.

Another old school aspect I was smartened up to at the academy was Ribs. Ribbing 101—an integral part of the Texas Wrestling Academy's curriculum. For the uninitiated, ribbing is all about playful pranks, a time-honored tradition in the wrestling world. Legends like Mr. Perfect, Curt Hennig, and Owen Hart have become synonymous with their mischievous antics, and in the realm of Texas wrestling, Rudy Boy Gonzalez was undoubtedly a master prankster, leaving an indelible mark in the history of ribbing.

As a young, impressionable 17-year-old, I was no stranger to pranks, having already dabbled in some playful mischief during my time playing sports in high school. So, when it came to ribbing at the Texas Wrestling Academy, let's just say I was in my element and aced my minor in the art of practical jokes.

But one vital lesson I quickly learned was that if you were brave enough to pull off a rib on someone, you had better be prepared to face the music—a receipt, as they say in wrestling lingo. A receipt meant that the recipient of the prank had every right to seek revenge and give you a taste of your own medicine. It was all in good fun, though, and part of the camaraderie that bound us together as a tight-knit wrestling family.

With Rudy Boy at the helm, the fun tradition of ribbing seeped into every corner of the Texas Wrestling Academy experience. Whether we were within the school's walls, under the glitzy wrestling show lights, or simply sharing post-practice meals at restaurants, the ongoing prank wars never seemed to end. It was a lively free-for-all, and literally, no one was off-limits. But honestly, that's what made it all the more memorable and special.

As an old-school wrestling academy, this playful ribbing served as an integral part of our team-building process. It strengthened the bonds between us, fostering a sense of being a team that ran deep. I never allowed the pranks to get under my skin, having experienced similar shenanigans during my time in high school sports. If anything, the ribbing added an extra layer of excitement and laughter to our shared journey in the world of professional wrestling.

Since I embarked on my training journey from scratch, my focus shifted entirely to the Texas Wrestling Academy. It meant bidding farewell to my matches with PWI and other wrestling companies, leaving me in a matchless state for well over three months. Every single day, I poured my heart and soul into the academy, working out with relentless determination to elevate myself as a professional wrestler.

Then, like a glimmer of hope in the dark, Rudy Boy offered me an opportunity—a shot at wrestling in a show at Southwest Texas State University, now known as Texas State University. This show, for his wrestling promotion Extreme Texas Wrestling was held in the student courtyard, would serve as a dress rehearsal for me. The anticipation was nerve-wracking since I hadn't stepped into the ring for quite some time. But destiny had its plan, and I was about to find out.

The big day finally came on September 26, 2002. As I stepped into the spotlight, I couldn't help but feel butterflies dancing in my stomach. I honestly can't recall who my opponent was at that time, but what mattered most was the experience. The dedication I had put into training at Rudy Boy's Texas Wrestling Academy paid off splendidly. The rigorous training regimen, five days a week, wrestling with the same crew, fostered an incredible bond. We knew each other's body language, our moves, and limitations inside out. The familiarity with each other from training so much translated into a seamless and unforgettable performance on the Southwest Texas State University stage. It was as if we could wrestle with our eyes closed. The match flowed smoothly, leaving both the audience and me with a sense of fulfillment.

The difference between training at Rudy Boy's academy and my previous experiences at ACW was night and day. Back then, training sessions were sporadic, and the level of familiarity among the wrestlers wasn't nearly as cohesive. But now, at the Texas Wrestling Academy, I had found my place—a community of wrestlers committed to pushing each other to reach new heights. It was an environment where the passion for wrestling thrived, and the dreams we chased felt within reach.

Rudy's wrestling promotion, Extreme Texas Wrestling, became a badge of honor for me. Their events were held at Sunset Station, a vibrant club located in downtown San Antonio, close to the famed Alamodome. The setup at Extreme Texas Wrestling was nothing short of impressive, leaving a lasting impression on all who attended.

It was at these shows that I had the privilege of crossing paths with a multitude of wrestlers hailing from different corners of Texas. Many of them were unfamiliar faces to me, having graced the rings up in the Dallas-Fort Worth area for promotions like Professional Championship Wrestling (PCW) in Arlington. And there were also those from Houston, including the renowned "Hot Stuff Hernandez", a name I had previously heard being mentioned on various Texas indy circuits. The first time I encountered Hernandez was brief, a passing moment during the hustle and bustle of a wrestling event at Sunset Station in 2003, eventually he become one of my best friends in the business.

Rudy's promotion had a roster filled with seasoned wrestlers who were all eager for opportunities to showcase their skills. The diversity among them was truly impressive—wrestlers of different shapes and sizes, each bringing their own unique flair to the ring. This mix of talent created a valuable melting pot that fostered a wide range of experiences and perspectives. My own wrestling journey was closely tied to Rudy's ETW, which eventually underwent a rebranding and became Texas Wrestling Entertainment (TWE).

My first taste of championship victory came in the tag team division at Rudy's promotion. Alongside my partner, Big Dogg, we faced off against the formidable team of Mike Dell and Showtime Summers on February 9th, 2005. The stage was set at the Trishway Entertainment Center in San Antonio, Texas, an arena buzzing with anticipation.

Teaming with Mike Dell against Showtime

Our tag team match followed the classic wrestling recipe, combining dynamic action with storytelling that resonated with the audience. But it was the ending that truly stole the show – a brilliantly executed twist that added an element of surprise to the proceedings. As the climax approached, I found myself pinning Showtime Summers while Mike Dell pinned Big Dogg. The referee, caught in the complexity of the moment, initiated the count. The crowd held its breath. Two opposite siding opponents were declared the tag champs in a weird angle that caught everyone off guard. This marked the start of something interesting at Rudy's promotion. Every time we defended the tag titles, things went haywire with screwy finishes that flipped the champs around. It was like a roller-coaster of surprises, and it definitely kept the crowd hooked.

Texas Tag Champs with Darin Childs as the Rock And Roll Nightmares

What made this whole thing stand out is that it marked my first championship win. And these titles at Rudy's had a history connected to the ones from the Texas Wrestling Alliance (TWA), a promotion I really admired. So, getting my hands on a belt that guys like American Dragon and Brian Kendrick had held was a big deal for me. I mean, I was a huge fan of TWA, so you can imagine how cool that felt.

Looking back, that victory meant more than just a title. It showed that hard work pays off and that even the wildest dreams can come true. Going from being a fan in the crowd to a champion in the ring was an incredible journey. It's one of those moments that every wrestler remembers – that first taste of being a champ, and all the emotions that come with it.

During my time at Rudy's promotion, we were on a roll with numerous shows. The frequency of events meant we got a lot of ring time, honing our skills through repetition. However, the downside was that not all of these matches were captured on camera. It's a bit regrettable, as some of those bouts were truly unforgettable. I wish I had visual records of those moments, but they remain lost in the depths of time.

Among the many matches, there's one that stands out for me, and it happened years later. It was a series of matches with a fellow student named Brett Thunder. Our chemistry in the ring was exceptional, and I have to say, those matches were some of the most enjoyable and satisfying moments. Brett had a solid skill set, and in my eyes, he was one of the most dependable wrestlers in our state. I saw a bright future ahead for him, and it was a privilege to share the ring with someone who had such potential.

There's this one match that really sticks out in my mind. It was a real banger, full of hard hits and intense action. We covered everything from technical wrestling to crazy spots and near falls that had the crowd on the edge of their seats. We went all out, giving it our all for a good 25 to 30 minutes.

In the end, Brett came out on top. I remember being in the ring after the match, still catching my breath and feeling the impact of the battle we just had. Then, out of the blue, Brett returned to the ring. He grabbed the mic and told everyone to hold on because he wanted us to shake hands. He said it was a damn good match, and we should acknowledge it.

I later found out that it wasn't just his idea. Rudy Boy Gonzales had actually sent Brett back out there to make sure we shook hands in front of everyone. He recognized how solid our match was and wanted us to show that respect to each other. It was a cool moment, knowing that RBG thought so highly of our match. And Brett's move to come back and say that on the mic, it meant a lot. It was an unexpected pat on the back, and it's a memory that always brings a smile to my face.

Getting the endorsement of our trainer, Rudy, meant the world to me. You see, Rudy's not just a trainer to us; he's like a father figure. Over the years, we've had our ups and downs, our moments of frustration and even the urge to strangle him. But I can't deny that the man knows wrestling like the back of his hand. So, when he stepped out and told us that our performance was solid, it hit deep. It was more than just a compliment; it was validation from someone who's been in the business for ages. He understands the ins and outs, the intricacies that make a match great. And for him to give his nod of approval, well, that felt like a big deal.

Me and RBG in 2019 at an AWR Event.

Those moments stick with you. They're the moments that remind you why you're in this business in the first place. It's not just about the showmanship or the moves; it's about the respect and recognition from those who've paved the way before you. So, yeah, even though Rudy and I might butt heads on occasion, I can't deny the impact he's had on my journey, and that endorsement will always be a badge of honor.

As I look back on my journey, I am forever grateful to Rudy Boy Gonzalez for providing me with the tools, knowledge, and unwavering support that have propelled me forward in the world of professional wrestling. His belief in me, coupled with the camaraderie and unique experiences at the Texas Wrestling Academy and Extreme Texas Wrestling, have been vital stepping stones on my path to success.

My time at Rudy's marked a significant restart in my wrestling journey. After moving on from ACW, a stint at PWI, and some time in the Indies, I was ready for a fresh start, a clean slate under Rudy Boy's guidance. It was a decision to temporarily step away from active wrestling elsewhere, all in the pursuit of retraining, refining, and rejuvenating my skills. The hiatus from the ring was an investment in myself. It allowed me to polish up my techniques and truly grasp the basics of wrestling, establishing a solid foundation to build upon. Rudy's training wasn't just about flashy moves; it was about understanding the essence of the sport, the nuances that make a match compelling. And under his guidance, I found myself finally grasping these core elements.

But the journey was far from over. Armed with these newfound skills, I needed to put in the work, to get the reps in and truly develop my character. The wrestling ring is where theory meets reality, where all the training comes to life. It's in those moments of actual combat, those sweaty and intense matches, that a wrestler hones their craft. And at Rudy's, that's exactly what I set out to do. So, while my journey took me through different promotions and stages, it was at Rudy's that I rediscovered the essence of wrestling. It was here that I started with a clean slate, eager to learn, and committed to becoming the best version of myself in that squared circle.

So, thank you, Rudy, for being a guiding light in my wrestling career. You have left an enduring impact on me, and I carry your teachings and the cherished memories of our time together in every ring I step into.

Chapter 6
Wrestling's Evolution:
Choosing Ring Lights Over Prom Night

Wrestling today has evolved in ways that I couldn't have imagined when I first started in 2001. Sometimes, I can't help but feel like an old head, reminiscing about the days gone by. I remember listening to the veterans in the '80s talk about the importance of storytelling in the ring, using proper psychology, and grabbing a hold. Now, I find myself passing on the same wisdom to the younger generation, encouraging them to slow down, focus on the story, and use classic wrestling techniques.

It's amusing to see how the business has changed, and I wonder what my 2001 self would think if they saw me now. Back then, WWE was still WWF, and WCW and ECW were still in existence. The local wrestling scene had an old school mentality, emphasizing tough love and learning from mistakes. Dusting yourself off and trying again was the norm.

Some people argue that the old school approach is outdated, but I believe it's what made money on a local level. Looking back at the days of Southwest Championship Wrestling or the Texas Wrestling Alliance, wrestlers were brought up in a completely different way than what we see today.

However, I don't want to be the bitter grizzled veteran who criticizes everything about the modern wrestling scene. There's nothing inherently wrong with the way things are done now. Wrestling has evolved, and I respect the changes and the new talents that bring their unique styles and innovations to the ring.

Over my two decades in the wrestling business, I've learned a lot from my own mistakes, and now I strive to help others do the same. The stories you've read so far in this autobiography cover only the first two or three years of my wrestling career, and there are many more experiences I could share, but it would make this book immensely bigger.

In wrestling, how you react to what happens to you is crucial. If you face challenges or rough times, it's all about finding ways to improve, have better matches, get in better shape, and develop a stronger character. This mindset is something I try to instill in anyone who comes to me with questions or seeks advice.

Wrestling Psycho Simpson in one of my first ETW Matches

Back in the day, the older vets might have seemed scary and grizzled, and some were definitely a bit rough around the edges. However, they never steered me wrong, and I understood that tough love was part of their way of passing on valuable knowledge. Nowadays, it sometimes seems that some young wrestlers feel they're beyond criticism and don't need tough love. Unfortunately, this perspective can lead to labeling any constructive criticism as toxic.

When I first entered the business, it was a different world. The wrestling business was heavily protected, and as a rookie, I was kept in the dark about many things. Being a 17-year-old kid still in high school, I was often treated with skepticism, and some didn't believe I would last long. Back then, I found myself sitting in the back, surrounded by seasoned wrestlers who had previously made money in the wrestling circuit. I was instructed to stay quiet, listen, and learn, and I did my best to absorb every bit of knowledge.

Throughout the years, there were countless moments when people tried to make me quit, or I felt like giving up. However, I refused to let myself quit, and I persevered. Every interaction I had with someone in the wrestling business became a learning opportunity for me. I firmly believe that learning from every single person who has crossed my path in this business has been invaluable to my growth and success.

Sadly, it seems that this aspect of learning and respect has gotten lost in translation, especially in today's social media age. Nowadays, people tend to communicate mostly through their devices, venting their frustrations and complaints on social media, often revealing too much in the process. Back in the day, it was considered taboo to take pictures backstage or interact too openly with others. Now, you see wrestlers thanking each other for matches publicly on platforms like Facebook, taking photos together, and even sharing dream lists of opponents.

I remember when MySpace was a new thing, and even then, the business was still well-guarded, and you didn't see as much being exposed on social media. Unlike the current wrestling landscape, where wrestlers frequently share behind-the-scenes glimpses, engage in public interactions with other wrestlers, and openly discuss their matches and aspirations, the wrestling community back then operated with a different code of conduct. There was a sense of mystique and exclusivity surrounding the business. Backstage was considered sacred ground, and unauthorized photography or sharing of such content was frowned upon.

In those days, wrestlers learned the art of storytelling, in and out of the ring, through personal experiences and interactions with veterans. They honed their craft by carefully observing and imitating those who came before them, respecting the traditions and unwritten rules of the industry. It was a time when wrestlers guarded their characters and held back from breaking the illusion for fans.

As time went on, the advent of social media transformed the wrestling landscape dramatically. Wrestlers began to connect directly with their fans, sharing glimpses of their lives outside the ring and building personal brands. While this has undoubtedly brought fans and wrestlers closer together, it has also exposed the business in ways that were once inconceivable.

Training in the past was taken more seriously, and there was a strong emphasis on attending regular practices and putting in the hard work. Back then, if you weren't committed to training and showing up consistently, you were less likely to get booked on shows. It was a way to ensure that wrestlers were well-prepared and had the necessary skills before stepping into the ring for live events.

Back in those old school days, making wrestling your top priority was ingrained in us from the get-go, no matter the circumstances. It didn't matter if it was your birthday, your mom's birthday, a friend's wedding, or even your prom night – if you were booked for a show, you had to be there. That mentality was hammered into us repeatedly, and it became a way of life, though looking back, it did come with its sacrifices.

There were many precious moments with loved ones that I missed out on due to this strict commitment to wrestling. Friends and family on the outside couldn't always understand why I had to put wrestling above everything else. In hindsight, I can see how it affected my personal life, but at the time, I believed in the old school philosophy – for better or worse.

The old saying "every pencil has an eraser" was drilled into us, meaning there was no room for excuses. If you gave any kind of reason to an old timer, your name would be erased, and opportunities could be lost. Back then, making excuses simply wasn't an option, and you had to adapt and be ready for anything that the wrestling business threw at you.

Let me share a moment that truly showcases just how deeply the old-school mentality had me in its grip. Cast your mind back to a time when I was convinced I held the conductor's baton to the orchestra of my own life. In the annals of history, there's a story that stands as a testament to the rigid convictions I held, especially about never bailing on a commitment, no matter what.

So, here's where the hilarity – and my absurd decision-making skills – come into play. My girlfriend at the time Marie Matlock's senior prom was fast approaching, and as luck would have it, it fell on the very same night as one of my wrestling gigs. You'd think this would be a no-brainer, right? Wrong. Enter my stubborn, old-school mentality that screamed, "You never back out of a commitment, no matter what!"

With a heart full of misguided determination, I looked at the situation and thought, "Why not have my cake and eat it too?" So, I did the unthinkable. On May 19th, 2007 yours truly convinced his girlfriend Marie to come to my wrestling show, dolled up in her prom attire, makeup on point and everything. Can you imagine the scene? A wrestling crowd getting an unexpected taste of prom night elegance as Marie sat there among the hollering fans.

The highlight? I wrestled in the first match of the night, so while I was brawling in the ring, she was chilling in the audience, likely wondering if she'd stepped into an alternate dimension. I can only hope that the enthusiastic crowd reactions helped distract her from my in-ring antics.

But fear not, my fellow adventurers in poor judgment, I didn't leave her hanging. Post-match, I engaged in the quickest superhero transformation you've ever seen, swapping my sweaty wrestling gear for a hastily thrown-on tuxedo in record time. And then, off we dashed to her senior prom, like some bizarre Cinderella story, if Cinderella had a penchant for headlocks and suplexes.

Photo from my first prom in 2003 with Jeremy and Edwin

Looking back, was it the brightest decision? Not even close. I may have been taught to honor commitments, but I also learned that there's a time and place for everything — and prom night is definitely not a place for arm drags and body slams. Yet, in a twist of fate, Marie took it all in stride, and our night eventually turned into a story that never fails to draw laughter and eye rolls whenever it's recounted.

It's astonishing to think about the extent to which I was ingrained in the wrestling business, with its old-school values firmly rooted in my mind. There's one episode that vividly illustrates just how deep that commitment ran.

Imagine this: Marie, my girlfriend at the time, was on the cusp of her senior prom night. And then there was me, four years removed from my own high school graduation, fully convinced that missing a wrestling booking was out of the question. It's a memory that simultaneously makes me shake my head in disbelief and chuckle at the sheer audacity of my decision-making.

This particular prom turned out to be quite the memorable affair. Given that Marie and I shared the same high school, my presence at a prom four years after my own graduation was enough to raise a few eyebrows among the teachers. At the time, I was 22, and Marie was 18, so legality wasn't an issue, in case anyone's wondering.

The perplexed expression on one of my former teachers' faces when they asked me what brought me to the prom was priceless. My simple response? "I'm here with Marie." The night was an absolute blast, much more enjoyable than my own prom experience four years earlier. There was an added layer of amusement in seeing the teachers and staff trying to decipher why I, a graduate from years back, was mingling at the event.

Of course, times have changed, and the business has evolved to be more accommodating to individual circumstances. Promoters and wrestlers understand the importance of work-life balance, and that's a positive development. It's essential to prioritize personal responsibilities and family time when necessary.

Even so, the old school mentality instilled valuable qualities in us, like discipline, adaptability, and resilience. The wrestling business was indeed tougher back then, and the lesson that it owes you nothing was crystal clear. Things could change in an instant, and you had to be prepared to roll with the punches and adjust your plans accordingly.

Times have changed, and with the evolution of the wrestling business, some aspects have become more relaxed. While it's true that there are advantages to the current era, such as easier access to technology and the ability to share matches online effortlessly, it also comes with its own set of challenges.

Back in the day, you had to physically record your matches on VHS tapes and send them out by mail, hoping that the promoter would take the time to watch them. Today, with digital platforms and social media, sharing your matches and getting noticed by promotions is much more convenient and instantaneous. It has undoubtedly opened up new opportunities for aspiring wrestlers to showcase their talent and reach a broader audience.

However, the ease of sharing matches online has also led to a saturation of talent and, as I mentioned, some wrestlers getting in the ring before they are fully ready. It's important to strike a balance and ensure that proper training and dedication to the craft are still valued, even in this technology-driven era.

Throughout my wrestling career, I've witnessed the industry undergo remarkable changes, especially with the advancements in technology. One significant transformation lies in merchandise production. Back in the day, creating something as simple as an 8x10 photo required dealing with real film and hoping it turned out well. Nowadays, all it takes is a cell phone, some digital editing in programs like Photoshop, and a quick visit to a place like Walgreens to have high-quality prints ready in no time.

As I reflect on my journey, I can't help but feel like one of the last representatives of an old-school era. When I started, the wrestling landscape was already experiencing shifts due to WWE acquiring WCW and ECW, followed by the emergence of TNA Wrestling and Ring of Honor. The result was an explosion of Indie wrestling promotions, drawing in more aspiring professional wrestlers.

When I began my wrestling journey, there were only a couple of wrestling schools in the entire city of San Antonio. Fast forward to today, and there are at least five schools, signifying how the business has become more open and accessible to a broader range of aspiring wrestlers. While some may view this change skeptically, I acknowledge that it has its merits, making the industry more diverse and inclusive.

One of the most significant changes I've witnessed is the accessibility of wrestling knowledge. Back in the day, training was taken extremely seriously, and there was a sense of exclusivity around the business. Only a few lucky individuals had the chance to learn from seasoned veterans, and training was often grueling and demanding. But today, aspiring wrestlers have a wealth of resources at their fingertips – from online tutorials to video libraries of classic matches. While this has led to a wider pool of talent, it has also resulted in some inexperienced individuals getting in the ring before they are truly ready.

I can't help but marvel at how much the business has opened up and become more inclusive. Back when I started, the idea of intergender wrestling was almost unheard of, and women had limited opportunities in the industry. But now, women's wrestling has flourished, and we see talented female wrestlers headlining shows, winning championships, and proving themselves as equals to their male counterparts.

The emphasis on high-flying and high-risk maneuvers has also increased in recent years. While these acrobatic displays are undoubtedly impressive and thrilling to watch, I often find myself reminding younger wrestlers of the importance of telling a compelling story in the ring. Sometimes, less is more, and the art of wrestling lies in building tension, connecting with the audience, and taking them on a roller-coaster ride of emotions.

Let me clarify that I'm not trying to create a "back in my day" manifesto when discussing how the wrestling business has changed. I have an unwavering love for professional wrestling, and like any wrestler, I do have moments of reflection and a few regrets about my career. But that's only natural because we all strive to be the best in this business.

Entering the world of wrestling in 2001 was an incredible experience, especially as a teenager. It was a wild ride in a sport where veterans had witnessed and experienced so much. Learning from these seasoned wrestlers was invaluable; they not only taught me the ropes in the ring but also how to be a man and navigate life outside of wrestling.

The changes in the wrestling industry have been significant, but my admiration for the sport remains steadfast. I'm not here to resist progress or romanticize the past. Instead, I embrace the new opportunities and challenges that come with an evolving landscape. As the business shifts, so do the approaches, and I'm determined to stay adaptable and continually improve my craft.

Reflecting on my journey, I feel immensely blessed to have started in a time when wrestling was still guarded, and veterans played a prominent role in shaping young talent. The tough love and mentorship I received have left a lasting impact on me. They instilled values of respect, hard work, and perseverance that extend far beyond the wrestling ring.

In the early days of my wrestling journey, I was that eager kid who would do whatever it took to be a part of this business. Sneaking into bars and holding a drink to avoid suspicion, going on road trips to different cities on school nights just for a chance to wrestle, and even skipping football practice to attend wrestling training – I was hungry for every opportunity to learn and grow in the wrestling world.

As the wrestling landscape evolved, so did I. The experiences I gained in the ring and on the road shaped not just my career but also my character. Wrestling taught me resilience, discipline, and the importance of perseverance. It was a constant reminder that hard work, dedication, and a passion for what you do are the keys to achieving greatness.

Looking back now, I can't help but feel a sense of pride for the journey I've taken in the wrestling business. From that eager kid with dreams in his eyes to the seasoned wrestler standing tall today, the evolution has been incredible. Wrestling has gifted me with unforgettable memories, lifelong friendships, and a sense of purpose that transcends the squared circle.

As time passed and life unfolded, I had to adapt to the realities of adulthood, which led to some adjustments in my wrestling pursuits. I couldn't maintain the same level of intensity as before, but that didn't mean my passion for wrestling waned. On the contrary, I learned valuable life lessons along the way that extended beyond the squared circle.

The experiences I gained during my early years in wrestling helped shape the person I am today. Wrestling taught me discipline, perseverance, and the importance of commitment to my craft. These principles stayed with me as life's responsibilities grew, and I had to find a balance between my personal life and my wrestling career.

While I might not go on as many road trips anymore or attend every single training session anymore, my dedication to wrestling remains strong. I cherish those early memories of hunger and determination, as they laid the foundation for my journey. As I look back, I am grateful for the lessons learned and the memories made, and I know they have all contributed to making me the wrestler and the person I am today.

Writing this autobiography has been a truly enjoyable experience. Recollecting my thoughts and reminiscing about my journey in this business has evoked both nostalgic and emotional moments. As I wrote these first five chapters, I found myself reflecting on the significant milestones and challenges I faced, and it's an opportunity for me to share my experiences with readers.

In the midst of crafting this book, I am in the 22nd year of my pro wrestling career, and at 39 years of age, I can't help but contemplate the time I have left in this business. But as I delve deeper into writing, I realize that this book will be an assortment of various moments from my career, not necessarily presented chronologically. Instead, I want to share the most interesting and impactful moments that I believe will captivate and engage my audience.

My hope is that through reading this book, you'll gain a deeper understanding of the wrestling world. I want to offer insights into the joys, struggles, and dedication it takes to thrive in this captivating and ever-evolving industry. Whether you're an aspiring wrestler, a wrestling fan, or simply curious about the life of a pro wrestler, I aim to provide you with an authentic and compelling glimpse into this business that has shaped my life in ways I never could have imagined.

Chapter 7
The Unintended Legacy of 'The Dude Who Wrestles Girls'

In the early 2000s Texas wrestling scene, female wrestlers were a rarity, and unfortunately, not all of them were adequately trained. Often, they were added to shows as mere eye candy for the male-dominated audience. Upon joining Extreme Texas Wrestling (ETW) and learning under Rudy Boy Gonzalez's guidance, I experienced a shift. Starting in 2003, I had the privilege to step into the ring with a few well-established female wrestlers, one of them being Char Starr, the NWA women's world champion.

Char Starr was indeed a force to be reckoned with in the Texas wrestling scene. As the reigning women's champion in various promotions, she had established herself as the top female star in the region. Her towering presence and impressive muscular build were awe-inspiring, making the idea of her facing off against a relatively smaller and lighter wrestler like myself seem almost comical.

But in the world of wrestling, that's where the magic happens. It was all about creating intriguing and entertaining match ups that captured the imagination of the audience. The contrast between her dominance and my smaller stature added an element of excitement and curiosity to any in-ring interaction between us two.

One notable segment during an ETW show had me interrupting Char Starr's entrance and cutting a promo against women in wrestling. I remember that moment vividly - my first time grabbing the microphone and facing a roaring crowd! I was determined to make it unforgettable, but also a bit nervous about how it would be received. I knew I had to deliver something that would get a reaction, and boy, did I go all out!

I carefully crafted my promo, making sure to include every wild and outrageous thing I could say about women and wrestling, while keeping it clean and free of cuss words. It was all in good fun, and I wanted to push the boundaries of what was considered acceptable in the wrestling world at the time.

The crowd was in for a shock! You see, back in 2003 and 2004, it was rare to see men and women competing against each other in wrestling. It was a whole new territory, and I was ready to make my mark. The crowd loved it as we engaged in a brief altercation, and Char Starr eventually delivered her signature move, the X Factor, to send them home happy.

Interestingly enough, around this juncture, I found myself dating someone who shared my passion for wrestling. Her name was Nicole, known in the ring as Nayati, and she hailed from Houston. We initially connected online, and as our conversations deepened, our relationship took root. Eventually, she made the decision to move to San Antonio to be closer to me, solidifying our bond.

Our dynamic took a unique turn – whenever one of us received a booking, the other would invariably tag along. This arrangement not only strengthened our connection but also allowed us to feature on each other's shows. Over time, Nicole honed her skills impressively, becoming a noteworthy presence both in our matches and during training sessions at Rudy's.

In the wrestling world of that era, female wrestlers were a rarity, and Nicole stood out as one of the shining stars. It was a fascinating experience when we had to square off against each other in the ring. Far from holding back, we brought our full force to those matches, delivering hard-hitting moves that echoed our shared commitment to the sport.

As I ventured out to wrestle for other promotions, including George De La Isla's Capital of Texas Pro Wrestling (CTPW) in Austin, I found myself regularly facing women in the ring. Intergender matches were uncommon at that time, and I became known as the guy who wrestled women, which led to some ridicule and laughter from peers and fans alike. However, I took pride in being a trailblazer for this unique style of wrestling, providing opportunities for women to improve their skills by competing against male wrestlers.

Wrestling a member of the opposite sex was initially intimidating, but the suspension of disbelief in the wrestling world allowed for storytelling opportunities. I would often portray a chauvinistic pig, making it easy for the crowd to root against me, and wrestling became all about telling compelling stories.

Early in my wrestling journey, I found myself engaged in an intergender feud alongside Darin Childs, together forming the tag team known as "The Rock and Roll Nightmares." On August 21st, 2004, our opponents were two local female wrestlers, and the matches carried a high-stakes twist: if we were defeated, we'd have to wear dresses until we reclaimed a victory, while a loss for the women meant consuming dog food. This particular stipulation was quite old-school and raised eyebrows at the time, given that male-female wrestling match ups weren't common. Despite the unconventional setup, the feud turned out to be remarkably entertaining, and it even became a recurring element of my persona beyond my involvement in ETW. And just to clear things up, Darin and I ended up losing the match, leading to a stretch of time where we had to wrestle while wearing dresses.

Teaming up with Darin as "The Rock and Roll Nightmares" was a match made in wrestling heaven. Darin's old-school mentality perfectly complemented my passion for pushing boundaries and trying new things in the ring. Together, we formed a dynamic duo that helped pioneer intergender wrestling in the Texas wrestling scene of that time.

Lost a loser wears a dress tag match against women.

What set Darin apart was his fearlessness. He wasn't afraid to take bumps or experiment with innovative moves, making him the perfect partner to explore this uncharted territory. As a team, we embraced the challenge of facing off against women in the ring, and it quickly became one of the most exciting and enjoyable parts of my wrestling career.

The Rock And Roll Nightmares

Our chemistry and teamwork were evident to both our fans and opponents, and it didn't take long for us to capture Tag Team Championship gold. We relished the opportunity to feud with other tag teams across Texas, but it was when we faced women in the ring that we truly shined.

My journey in intergender wrestling continued to evolve as a result, and I found myself facing a diverse array of female opponents with varying skill levels. Some were fully trained and adept at putting on a great match, while others were thrown into the ring without much experience. Regardless of who I wrestled, I embraced each opportunity as a chance to grow and improve as a performer.

One memorable match was against a wrestler named Cherry Pie on February 20th, 2004. Rather than the traditional wrestling bout, the concept was a comedic approach where I portrayed a suitor trying to impress her. Throughout the match, anytime she applied a wrestling hold, I pretended to enjoy it, adding a humorous twist to the encounter. Although she might not have been the most technically skilled wrestler, Cherry Pie knew how to entertain the crowd, and the match turned out to be a fun and enjoyable experience.

But when my girlfriend at the time Nicole saw the match, she didn't quite appreciate the "flirting" aspect of it. She thought I was having a little too much fun, not realizing that it was all scripted and part of the story line. I tried explaining to her that I was just doing what the promoter and booker asked of me, but she couldn't shake off the jealousy.

Now, let me give a piece of advice to anyone in the wrestling business who has a jealous partner: communication is key! If you ever decide to take part in intergender matches or any story line that might raise eyebrows, be sure to give your partner a heads up. Explain that it's all part of the entertainment and that it doesn't reflect how you feel in real life.

Navigating a romantic relationship within the wrestling world, especially at the grassroots level, can prove to be a challenging endeavor. Multiply that challenge by tenfold if your partner is also a fellow professional wrestler. The dynamics at play are complex, often requiring you to contend with amplified levels of jealousy and insecurity.

In the realm of wrestling, where the interactions are frequent and the camaraderie runs deep, there's a plethora of variables that can fuel these emotions. The issue of trust looms large, as the constant presence of others in the industry can spark concerns about potential flirtations or interactions. It's important to realize that the nature of wrestling fandom often leads to admiration and attraction toward both you and your partner.

Undeniably, this phenomenon can be a harsh truth to accept. However, a crucial aspect of maintaining a healthy relationship in the wrestling world is cultivating mutual trust and assurance. If doubt lingers or if faithfulness is a topic of concern, it's an indication that perhaps being in a relationship within the wrestling scene might not be the best fit.

I have distinct memories of occasions when Nicole would experience bouts of jealousy stemming from something I did during a match. It was puzzling to me, as I've always approached my interactions with female wrestlers within the ring with a clear conscience and devoid of any malicious or suggestive intent. Despite my genuine intentions, I found myself frequently facing accusations and mistrust throughout our relationship.

The reality of constantly being under such scrutiny was a challenge, one that persisted throughout the entirety of our time together. It was as if the assumption of ulterior motives colored her perspective, even though my actions were driven purely by my commitment to the wrestling craft. This consistent strain on our relationship made it all the more challenging to navigate the already intricate world of pro wrestling.

As time unfolded, our relationship eventually came to an end, years down the line. Interestingly, it was revealed that it was she who had not upheld her end of the fidelity agreement. This revelation was a blow to my heart, as I had always been a devoted and committed partner, striving to give my best. I loved her.

Getting through the breakup wasn't easy. We had a lot of mutual friends and mentors in the business, which made things messy. It was also tough because she was my first real relationship and I fell hard for her. Dealing with the aftermath of the split brought on a ton of anxiety, especially being around people during shows. I actually started getting sick and puking before matches from all the nerves. It took me to a really dark place and pushed me into a deep depression. That whole experience made me swear off dating anyone in the business again – I realized it just wasn't worth the toll it was taking on my mental health.

The experience was a stark reminder that the realm of wrestling relationships carries inherent risks. The ever-present possibility of misunderstandings, doubts, and the tinge of jealousy can strain even the most well-intended partnerships. Being in the wrestling industry adds an extra layer of complexity to romantic relationships, as it often amplifies insecurities and exacerbates doubts.

Sadly, dating within the wrestling world triggered some personal insecurities for me. These feelings had a lasting impact, shaping my attitude and interactions in future relationships. This experience ingrained a certain negativity in me, which affected how I approached new relationships even those outside of wrestling. Despite the eventual ending of our relationship, I can't deny that she was an exceptional women's wrestler. Her determination and passion for the sport were truly impressive, and I took immense pride in witnessing her accomplishments during the time we were together.

As intergender wrestling became more accepted over time, I felt a sense of pride in being ahead of the curve in Texas wrestling. Embracing this unique style allowed me to create entertaining and engaging stories that captivated the audience. While some might have criticized me for wrestling women, I saw it as an opportunity to showcase the athleticism, talent, and dedication of female wrestlers.

I must admit that early on, I had my reservations about the concept, but I soon realized that the wrestling world is all about pushing boundaries and challenging preconceived notions. Intergender wrestling provided an exciting avenue to explore, creating scenarios that captivated the fans and allowed female wrestlers to shine.

In today's wrestling landscape, intergender matches have become more common, and the reception from the fans has been overwhelmingly positive. I cherish the memories and experiences from my intergender wrestling journey and take pride in my contribution to the growth and acceptance of this unique style.

Wrestling women in those days presented unique challenges as there was no set formula for making it believable. It required creativity and improvisation to deliver entertaining and engaging matches. Over time, I mastered the art of wrestling females, and these matches became some of the most enjoyable and fun experiences of my career.

As the years passed, I witnessed positive changes in women's wrestling, and I am proud to have played a role in paving the way for intergender wrestling. Today, intergender matches have become more commonplace, and I continue to wrestle women, cherishing the opportunity to entertain the fans while showcasing the progress and empowerment of women in the wrestling industry.

Despite initial skepticism and criticism, I embraced the evolution of women's wrestling, and deep down, I take pride in contributing to its growth. I may play the chauvinistic character in the ring, but in reality, I respect and appreciate the incredible strides women have made in wrestling over the last two decades. It's a testament to their skill, dedication, and passion for the sport that intergender wrestling has become a celebrated and integral part of today's wrestling landscape.

Admittedly, wrestling against women doesn't always turn out smooth. In fact, one of the worst matches I've ever been a part of unfolded on September 22nd, 2007, in Fort Riley, Kansas. Despite putting in genuine effort and working hard, things just didn't fall into place. The choreography, the coordination—everything about the match seemed to be going off track. The end result was nothing short of a chaotic mess.

I vividly recall the bell ringing to start the match, and as we moved to tie up, the girl's expression resembled that of a deer caught in headlights. She appeared utterly lost, trying her best to adapt on the fly. It was a struggle, and the situation felt magnified as if we were under a microscope, with everything seemingly going wrong. About midway through, we managed to find a bit of a rhythm, but I had heard from others, including fellow female wrestlers, that this girl often had moments of mental lapses during her matches. Let me be clear, there's no disrespect intended towards her whatsoever—she's an incredible person.

Surprisingly, the audience was still quite engaged, which only made the situation more surreal. It's a match that stands out in my memory as a drizzling mess, to put it lightly. Adding to the interesting mix of emotions, I recall that a former WCW star, Disco Inferno, was on the same show. As I made my way backstage after the match, he quipped, "Well, that was something," and walked away.

That moment is etched in my memory. Being a devoted WCW fan, Disco Inferno stood out as one of my favorites. His numerous championships and consistent in-ring performances earned him that spot. His advice on that day left a lasting impact, teaching me the vital lesson that in certain cases, less is more.

Me vs Alyssa Flash in 2010 after our first match.

With all this nostalgia and discussion about women's wrestling, I cannot have a chapter about wrestling women if I don't talk about the most notable feud of my entire career. In the scorching summer of 2010, my home base promotion at the time dropped a bombshell on me - I was going to kick off a feud with none other than Alyssa Flash.

If you're not familiar with her, Alyssa Flash was a world-renowned women's wrestler, ranked as the best in the world at one point by Pro Wrestling Illustrated. She had previously wrestled under different names like Cheerleader Melissa and Raisha Saeed in Impact Wrestling, and let me tell you, she was a legit bad ass. In my humble opinion, there probably wasn't a better women's wrestler on the entire planet than Alyssa.

I couldn't contain my excitement about going head-to-head with her in the ring. Eager to size up my formidable opponent, I watched some of her previous matches against male competitors, and boy, was I blown away! This girl was tough as nails, engaging in some of the most brutal intergender matches I had ever seen. She was literally lifting men up, suplexing them into chairs, body-slamming them on the floor, and tossing guardrails on top of them like it was a schoolyard brawl. Alyssa Flash was the epitome of a fearless and dominant competitor, and I knew right then and there that this feud was going to be pure gold.

With the knowledge of her prowess, my determination to bring my A-game was unwavering. I was ready to give it my all in the ring, knowing that this feud was destined to be a main event spectacle. The anticipation built up as I envisioned captivating audiences and pushing the boundaries of what intergender wrestling could be.

In our first match, the anticipation was palpable as we stepped into the ring. From the get-go, we engaged in a thrilling display of technical wrestling, exchanging hold for hold. Alyssa Flash proved to be a force to be reckoned with, quickly gaining the upper hand. She sent me flying with a body slam, and then, without hesitation, she wheelbarrowed me into the crowd, unleashing a relentless assault with the chairs and guardrails. The impact was so intense that the crowd fell into a stunned silence, unsure if what they were witnessing was part of the show or an all-out war.

Determined to retaliate, I introduced a steel chair into the equation, setting the stage for a devastating slam that landed Alyssa Flash right on top of it. The echo of her painful howl filled the air, leaving no doubt that this was a battle for the ages. Trust me when I say, I never dished out such a beating to a woman before, but I also never had anyone else hit me as hard as she did.

That first match was nothing short of legendary, standing out as one of the best in my entire career up to that point. It also marked a turning point for me, as it catapulted me into the spotlight of the main event scene in South Texas. After struggling to get over as a heel for years, I finally found my stride, and I owe a tremendous debt of gratitude to Alyssa Flash for helping me reach that pinnacle.

Following that incredible encounter, we received the exciting news that the feud would continue, and this time, the stakes were raised to unprecedented heights. It became official on July 3rd, 2010. For the very first time in indy wrestling history, a heavyweight championship belt would be up for grabs in an intergender match, with the possibility of it being held by a female competitor if Alyssa emerged victorious. It was groundbreaking, making waves across the wrestling world. Wrestling websites like Diva Dirt covered the events, recognizing the historical significance of a major championship being contested between a male and female competitor in an intergender match.

The possibility of making history added a new layer of intensity to our feud. The eyes of the wrestling world were upon us, and the pressure was on to deliver yet another epic showdown. The anticipation of what was to come electrified the air, and we were both determined to prove that intergender wrestling could be a showcase of skill, athleticism, and pure passion, regardless of gender.

The anticipation for our second match was off the charts, and this time it was officially for the heavyweight title. I held the championship going in, and my status as the hottest heel in the promotion had the crowd clamoring to see me get my comeuppance. I had garnered scorching heat, and fans would often try to fight me after shows. They'd turn their backs on me when I took the mic, and Alyssa Flash's desire to kick my ass only fueled their fervor, making them eager to buy tickets.

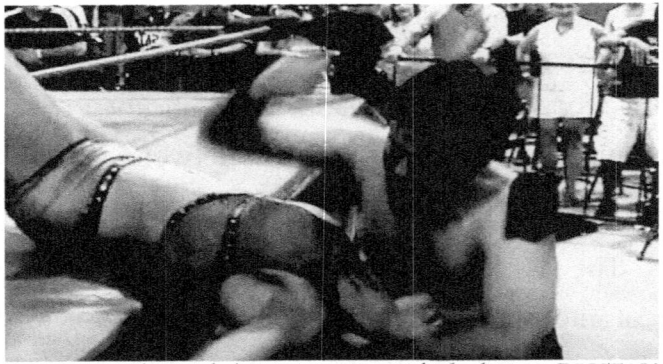

The second match between me and Flash was BRUTAL!

The second match proved to be even more intense than the first. Alyssa slammed me through chairs on the outside and hurled chairs at my head while I was against the wall. I retaliated, suplexing her into a trailer, and we spent a significant portion of the match fighting outside the ring. We beat the living hell out of each other, leaving it all on the line.

The stipulation added an extra layer of drama. Alyssa had 15 minutes to beat me for the championship. As the match reached its climax, she hit her finishing move and made the cover for what seemed like a three-count, and the crowd erupted in celebration. Alyssa held the title high, and everyone went home happy, celebrating her historic victory.

The news of this groundbreaking event trended on several wrestling websites, proclaiming that a woman wrestler had won a major heavyweight title in an independent promotion. But then, just three days later, what became known as "Black Monday" shook the wrestling world. The commissioner of the promotion announced that Alyssa Flash's pin came at 15 minutes and 3 seconds, three seconds too late to secure the championship. As a result, the title was returned to me.

The fallout from this twist was beyond anything I could have imagined. My social media was ablaze, fans were genuinely outraged, and the wrestling websites that had covered the historic moment were furious. We had them hooked, line, and sinker. It was a testament to the power of wrestling in captivating fans and having them suspend disbelief, investing wholeheartedly in our feud. To this day, I can confidently say that I have never seen such a level of fan investment in a feud at that promotion.

On August 7th, 2010, the scene was perfectly set for the third and final encounter of our remarkable feud. I, the reigning champion Joey "Supershot" Spector, would defend the championship against the formidable Alyssa Flash in what promised to be another hard-hitting encounter. As the day approached, excitement and anticipation filled the air, both among the fans and within the wrestling community.

The third match was unlike anything I had ever experienced before. It was a wild ride, filled with suspense, drama, and sheer brutality. I'll admit, I genuinely feared for my safety when I devised a devious plan. Two of my henchmen came to the ring, attacking Alyssa mercilessly, clubbing her in the back, and holding her as I landed brutal slaps. My intention was to provoke a riot, creating chaos and further fueling the intense atmosphere.

But my plan backfired when two of the top baby faces rushed to the ring, driving my henchmen away, and leaving me alone to face Alyssa Flash. She fired up, unleashing a flurry of chops and slams, and we fought all the way to the outside of the ring, out of the building, and even onto the back of a truck. In a moment of epic proportions, we crashed through a table, and the impact knocked her out momentarily. As she covered me for the three-count, the crowd erupted in awe.

It was a monumental moment in wrestling history as Alyssa Flash won the championship, and the crowd went home in awe of the spectacular match they had witnessed. The three-match feud had come to a close, leaving an indelible mark on the wrestling world. But the rivalry didn't end there. Alyssa and I continued to cross paths in various matches, including tag team and six-man tag matches. The intensity of our encounters never waned, and I even brought in Mercedes Martinez as my girlfriend in a quest for revenge.

Throughout it all, Alyssa Flash remained the ultimate professional. Despite her fearless and intense in-ring persona, she carried herself with utmost dedication and respect for the craft. She was one of my favorite opponents of all time, and I cherished every moment we shared in the squared circle.

My biggest rivalry - Alyssa Flash

To this day, I am grateful for everything Alyssa did for me and for the unforgettable matches we delivered. She was the Ricky Steamboat to my Ric Flair, a rival and partner in wrestling history, and our feud will forever be etched in the hearts of wrestling fans and professionals alike. The memories of those battles will always hold a special place in my heart, and I will forever appreciate the impact she had on my wrestling journey.

One of my dearest friends in the wrestling world is Baby D, a talented female wrestler. She portrayed a character of a "thick" girl who believed she was cute, and let me tell you, she absolutely nailed that gimmick. Her connection with the crowd was phenomenal, and she exhibited strong skills inside the ring as well. We had a series of matches together, and I must say, she had an impressive resilience. Taking a beating seemed to be her forte, and it wasn't surprising since she came from a wrestling lineage herself—being a second-generation wrestler, the business was practically in her blood.

Baby D was one of my favorite females to wrestle.

I have a distinct memory of a particular show on November 3rd, 2017 where we were booked in a fan Lumberjack match. This was a match type I was known for, and it involved fans surrounding the ring, armed with leather straps. If a wrestler fell out of the ring, the fans would unleash their wrath with those straps. It was an intense setup, but the energy and excitement it brought were electrifying.

Given my role as a heel, it was only natural that the fans would take the opportunity to unleash their aggression on me. This particular time, the dynamics were different—Baby D was playing the face, and unsurprisingly, they refrained from laying a hand on her. The intriguing twist came when I, as the heel, would toss her out of the ring during the match. It was all in good fun, of course. Each time I did so, I would turn to the crowd and taunt them, questioning why they wouldn't give her a taste of the leather straps they held.

As the match progressed, my antics escalated. I took hold of the referee, relieved him of his belt, and began to rain blows upon Baby D with an intensity that left no room for subtlety. I remember the moment vividly, and yes, my words lacked a filter. During the action, I even shouted, "I'm going to whip her harder than Jesus was whipped." Looking back, it's clear I was committed to my character, no matter how audacious it might have seemed.

On that particular evening, Jake "The Snake" Roberts graced us with his presence as a guest. It added an extra layer of excitement to the atmosphere as he observed the events unfold from backstage.

As the match reached its climactic moment, we decided to play with the possibility of Baby D striking me with a chair. The tension in the air was palpable. I seized the opportunity and kicked her in the gut, snatching the chair from her grasp. It was at that instant that I distinctly heard Jake The Snake's voice call out from behind the curtain, "Hit that bitch!"

With those words echoing in my ears, I reared back and delivered a powerful blow with the chair, the impact resounding through the arena. The connection was solid, and as the chair met its target, I capitalized on the moment and swiftly went for the pin fall. Baby D had a unique trait that set her apart—she wasn't one to shy away from the physicality of the sport. She wasn't afraid to take a hit, a quality that underscored her dedicated work ethic.

In a wrestling world often dominated by certain accepted standards of appearance, Baby D shattered those stereotypes. She didn't conform to the notion that one had to fit a particular mold, and that's what made her stand out. Her spirit and determination were evident in her hard work, both inside and outside the ring.

Despite the challenges, she carried herself with pride, breaking barriers and redefining what it meant to be a wrestler. Baby D holds a special place in my heart, forever etching her name as one of my cherished friends in this industry.

Chapter 8
Working with the Big Leagues:
Avoiding Bubba's Fury

As an indy wrestler, one of the most thrilling experiences is the chance to work as an extra when WWE comes to town. They often scout for local talent to fill roles such as security guards, EMTs or jobbers during segments. An unforgettable memory for me occurred in 2003 at WWE Survivor Series, held at the American Airlines Center in Dallas, Texas, on November 16th.

The excitement was palpable as this event took place shortly after the WWE Alliance story line ended. The roster was star-studded, featuring top names from

WWE, WCW, and ECW like Goldberg, Eddie Guerrero, Batista, Brock Lesnar, Big Show, Undertaker, Scott Steiner, Rob Van Dam, Booker T and many more. Being backstage for the first time and awaiting our instructions for the night was surreal.

Before we started, we had the opportunity to witness the behind-the-scenes preparations that go into producing such a spectacular WWE show. And here comes a crazy story from that night - meeting Mark Cuban, the billionaire owner of the Dallas Mavericks and the American Airlines Arena. At the time, I had no clue who he was, but he approached our group, introduced himself, and asked about our experience at the arena. It was later that I realized who he was when he appeared alongside Randy Orton during a practice session in the ring, demonstrating the RKO on a crash pad.

After the encounter with Mark Cuban, the excitement continued to build as Vince McMahon himself made his way to ringside. We were all eager to shake his hand, but he walked past us without acknowledging our presence. While it was intimidating to see him up close, it was also a fascinating experience to be within arm's distance of the man who has been instrumental in the growth of WWE and pro wrestling as we know it. Realistically, I didn't expect him to stop and chat, considering the magnitude of his responsibilities.

As more wrestlers began arriving, the energy in the arena area surged. Goldberg, Batista, Brock Lesnar, Albert, and several other big names walked by. Some of them jokingly remarked on our height, making us feel quite short in comparison. It's unclear if Goldberg's comment calling us "fucking midgets" was just playful banter or if he meant it rudely, but it left a vivid memory in my mind. To be fair, we were indeed a relatively short group, as Dean Malenko pointed out when he lined us up and individually assessed our heights, remarking on the obvious.

Despite not being selected to act as a security guard for the Stone Cold Steve Austin and Eric Bischoff fight, I was told to wait inside catering in case I would be needed for another role. The fact that we were still going to get paid for our time there was a great consolation and added to the overall awesomeness of the experience.

After not being chosen as security guards for the Stone Cold Steve Austin and Eric Bischoff fight, I found myself in the catering area, surrounded by other wrestlers like Shelton Benjamin, Paul London, Tommy

Dreamer, Rhino, and many more. In the big leagues, there was an unwritten rule: don't touch the catering, until everyone else actually employed by WWE eats, superstars, production crew or any other WWE employee. Despite being hungry and the catering spread looking impressive, I respected the tradition and waited until everyone had their share.

Observing how the professionals interacted with each other was a fantastic experience. Handshakes and cordial greetings were the norm, and the whole atmosphere was well-organized and professional. Witnessing the backstage production and the brotherhood among the wrestlers added to the awe of the event.

A funny moment occurred when Big Show grabbed five different plates and sat at different tables each time. It was amusing to see the gentle giant enjoying his meal in this unique manner. Tommy Dreamer also challenged Shelton Benjamin to scarf down a hot dog bun without drinking water, telling him it was impossible within a certain time frame.

Later, Dean Malenko returned and asked for two more people to play the role of EMTs, driving the ambulance during the Kane versus Shane street fight. Considering that he didn't want to overdo the number of security guards getting beat up, Malenko selected two individuals for the role.

That night, I found myself in one of the most embarrassing and nerve-wracking situations of my life. I had chosen to wear an Extreme Texas wrestling t-shirt, which was a blatant rip-off of the ECW logo. I didn't think it would be a problem, but as I sat in the back, I heard a loud booming voice calling out, "Hey Paul, do you see that guy wearing a shirt with your rip-off logo? I ought to rip that shirt off of him and beat the crap out of him." To my dismay, it was the Dudley Boyz and Paul Heyman standing about 20 feet away from me.

While Paul Heyman and Devon were laughing, Bubba seemed to be causing the commotion. I tried to act like I didn't hear them, desperately wishing I could just disappear at that moment. My nerves were getting the best of me, and I could feel myself shaking with anxiety. Feeling uneasy, I quickly walked away and coincidentally ran into Paul London.

Paul London, who I had previously known because he worked at Rudy's as well, could tell I was flustered and advised me to go into the bathroom and turn my shirt inside out for the rest of the night. It was a smart move to avoid any potential confrontation and enjoy the event without further trouble. Following his advice, I kept a low profile and made sure to steer clear of the Dudley Boyz for the rest of the night. As challenging as it was, the experience taught me a valuable lesson about being mindful of what I wear, especially in such a high-profile environment.

Fifteen years later, I had the opportunity to share this story with Devon Dudley. I got to work in an 8-man tag with him at a local promotion I was a part of. Not surprisingly, he had no recollection of the incident, but he chuckled and remarked that it sounded like something Bubba Ray would do. I vividly recalled how scared I felt when I heard Bubba Ray's booming voice threatening to kick my ass for wearing that shirt.

At the time, I couldn't tell if Bubba was just messing with me or genuinely upset, but either way, the encounter was quite intimidating. Looking back, it's a memory that still gives me chills, and sharing it with Devon Dudley added a humorous twist to the whole experience.

Several years down the line, on February 6th, 2010, I found myself presented with another thrilling chance to participate in a WWE House show held in Waco, Texas. For those unfamiliar with house shows, these are local live events that aren't filmed for television. This particular show featured CM Punk's stable, The Straight Edge Society, where he had been selecting individuals from the crowd to join his group by shaving their heads.

As I walked in, Fit Finlay welcomed me and informed me that they had something special planned for me that day. He asked if I had any experience taking bumps in the ring, and after confirming my experience, he revealed the unique role I would play. I was going to be the first person ever to refuse having my head shaved by CM Punk's group and, as a result, get beat up by Luke Gallows and CM Punk himself.

Though it wasn't a formal match, the opportunity was still thrilling. Getting inside the ring and being a part of the action, even in this capacity, was an incredible experience. The adrenaline rush and the chance to interact with the WWE superstars made it a memorable moment in my wrestling journey. I recall having to change into clothes that resembled those of a fan and then taking a seat at ringside, blending in seamlessly with the crowd. It was a fantastic experience being among the fans during the early part of the show.

When the moment arrived, CM Punk and Luke Gallows emerged to do their promo and search for a fan willing to volunteer for the head-shaving ritual. Without hesitation, I eagerly raised my hand and called out, "Me, me!" They selected me and invited me into the ring, where the real fun began.

Acting as if I had never been inside a wrestling ring before, I had to pretend not to know the basics of crawling to the ropes or any other fundamental moves. It was quite the challenge to convincingly portray a "mark" or an unsuspecting fan, but it made the experience all the more interesting and entertaining.

During the event, they seated me in a chair, and CM Punk, along with Luke Gallows, delivered a powerful speech about The Straight Edge Society's mission to promote a clean and positive lifestyle, avoiding alcohol and drugs. It was the same heartfelt message they had been conveying on TV at the time. They asked if I was ready for the head-shaving, and I initially agreed.

But, just as they were about to begin, I had a sudden change of heart and called out, "Wait a minute, wait a minute, I changed my mind!" But before I knew it, Luke Gallows delivered a thunderous big boot, sending me sprawling out of the chair. They proceeded to unleash a beat down on me, which certainly left an impact.

However, the moment took an unexpected turn when Rey Mysterio rushed to the ring. He came to my rescue, engaging in a thrilling spot with both Luke Gallows and CM Punk, ultimately saving the day and carrying me to the back. Being saved by one of my wrestling idols, especially as a Hispanic wrestler, was a surreal and unforgettable experience. It was undeniably one of the coolest things I've ever done in my wrestling journey.

While I wish the moment had been captured on television for everyone to see, unfortunately, it wasn't aired. It's a memory I hold dear, and I only wish my family had taken a picture since they were present at the event. Nonetheless, the memories of that incredible night remain etched in my mind, and I will cherish them forever.

I have a vivid memory of that particular house show for a specific reason – the interactions I had with Ricky Steamboat and CM Punk were truly memorable. Before the event, I had the opportunity to speak with Ricky Steamboat quite a bit, as I had previously attended a few clinics with him. I expressed my gratitude for his valuable guidance, and he was incredibly friendly and offered me more advice.

Throughout the day, I made sure to stay away from catering and changed in the stairwell instead, following the old school mentality that the WWE locker room was off-limits to me as an outsider. Although times may have changed, I stuck to the tradition of keeping a distance and respecting the space of the established wrestlers.

As a result, I hadn't eaten anything the entire day. After our spot in the ring with CM Punk, as I stood by the curtain, he noticed my empty stomach and asked why I hadn't eaten. I explained my reluctance to go into catering, and without hesitation, CM Punk took matters into his own hands. He firmly took hold of my wrist and brought me to catering, where he grabbed a Subway sandwich, split it in half, and shared it with me. He assured me that if anyone had an issue with it, they would have to come to him.

It was an incredible gesture of camaraderie and support from CM Punk, and I'll always remember his kindness. This day will forever be etched in my memory, and I often find myself wishing I could somehow reach out and reconnect with CM Punk. I'd love to remind him of that special moment and express my heartfelt gratitude for his kindness and support, not only during our interaction but throughout the rest of the night as well.

As the event unfolded, I had the privilege of engaging in conversations with several other roster members, and to my surprise, they were incredibly warm and friendly. Despite my nerves and the old school teachings that had shaped my approach, they made me feel welcome and valued as a part of the wrestling community.

If you are a wrestler seeking a chance to be an extra on a show, it's essential to find a way to contact the relevant authorities responsible for these opportunities. While it may rotate frequently, local wrestling schools often have priority in getting called first. I consider myself fortunate to have had the opportunity to be an extra on several occasions.

There was even a possibility for a third opportunity, but regrettably, I messed it up, leading to an embarrassing incident. This unfortunate event occurred just before Survivor Series 2003 when Steve Austin had left the company, and there were speculations about his return. Eric Bischoff designed a story line centered around finding Stone Cold Steve Austin, and the segments were filmed in Bandera, Texas, which is located close to San Antonio.

I remember vividly when Rudy called and told me he had secured a spot for me to be part of that skit. All I needed to do was wake up early at 5:30 in the morning and meet at a designated hotel in San Antonio. He emphasized keeping it a secret, which I respected.

However, I must admit, at that time, I was more of a night owl and had difficulty getting enough sleep. Waking up in the morning was always a challenge, and on this critical day, it worked against me. I won't make excuses; it was my mistake, and I take full responsibility for it. It wouldn't be an honest account of my wrestling journey if I didn't share my shortcomings and the lessons learned.

As fate would have it, I slept through my alarm and woke up at 8:00 am., feeling panicked and realizing my blunder. I rushed to the hotel, hoping against hope that I could catch up with the group. The front desk informed me that they had just left, but I still attempted to reach them by phone. Despite my numerous calls, nobody answered. Feeling the weight of my mistake, I decided to leave a handwritten letter for the producers at the hotel's front desk, explaining my situation and expressing my sincere regret.

Upon returning home, I received the news that my opportunity had slipped through my fingers, and an official confirmed my misstep over the phone. I cannot deny how utterly embarrassed I felt at that moment. But as they say, mistakes happen to the best of us, and this was certainly a humbling experience for me. It serves as a reminder that even in the world of wrestling, being responsible and making the most of every opportunity is crucial. It's essential to learn from our errors and strive to do better in the future.

Apart from my experiences with WWE, I've had the incredible opportunity to be an extra or enhancement talent in other promotions, such as Lucha Libre USA. A moment that's forever etched in my memory took place on May 11th, 2012, when I had the incredible opportunity to wrestle in the Alamodome. It truly was an awe-inspiring experience. Stepping into the ring and performing in front of thousands of people in such a massive arena was surreal. It felt incredible to engage with the audience and elicit boos as a heel, creating that special connection with the fans.

Additionally, we participated in a Battle Royal, adding to the excitement and adrenaline of the event. Lucha Libre USA also took their shows to baseball fields, including their event on May 12th, 2012, at Dell Diamond in Round Rock. These settings offered distinctive and enjoyable experiences for everyone involved.

The best part of these shows was the opportunity to interact with a diverse range of talent. I got to meet former WWE stars who were no longer under contract, as well as talented individuals from the independent wrestling scene, who were working hard to carve a name for themselves. The experience of being among the wrestlers and the chance to share the ring with such a talented pool of individuals made these shows all the more special.

In 2007 and 2008, I had an exciting working relationship with the NWA, facilitated by David Marquez. They would rent my ring for their arena events in South Texas, and this arrangement allowed me to tour with the NWA whenever they came to the region. It was an amazing opportunity as I got to be a part of the shows in various roles.

Sometimes, I had the privilege of refereeing the matches, and other times, I was fortunate enough to step into the ring as a wrestler. Carmine Despirito, David Marquez's right-hand man at the shows, played a pivotal role in orchestrating the events. At the time, I often found myself assigned as a referee, but my eagerness to wrestle was hard to contain. I frequently approached Carmine, expressing my interest and letting him know that I was more than capable of taking on a more active role. Refereeing, while important, didn't quite quench my thirst for being in the ring, and I was ready for more wrestling action.

I would follow Carmine around on show day, mentioning I had my gear to the point he would start avoiding me in a funny way. Then came that unforgettable moment that has etched its place in Joey Spector wrestling history. I asked once again, "is there a spot to wrestle tonight?" Carmine Despirito looked me straight in the eyes and without missing a beat dropped the bombshell, "Wrestle? What's all this wrestling bullshit? You're here to referee." To this day, whenever we cross paths, that legendary exchange resurfaces, and it's become our humorous way of saying hello. The memory of that frank, funny moment is a vivid reminder of how sometimes a single sentence can encapsulate so much.

Among all the wrestling experiences I've had, the one that stands out as my favorite occurred on April 15th, 2007, in Hidalgo, Texas, where we had a match at the Dodge Arena. The atmosphere was electric, and the house was nearly sold out, thanks to the presence of some big-time Lucha Libre stars on the show.

Wrestling in an arena that was packed with passionate fans made a significant difference in my performance. The energy and support from the audience made it much easier to connect with them, and I cherished every moment of it. If I had the chance to wrestle in such an environment regularly, I would seize it without hesitation. Another highlight was when we performed at the Freeman Coliseum in San Antonio. This venue holds a special place in wrestling history, having hosted numerous old school wrestling events over the years. Being part of that legacy was a truly humbling experience.

These events were nothing short of grand spectacles, marked by high production values that set them apart. Just consider the arenas they took place in—

names like the Alamodome and the Freeman Coliseum immediately come to mind. These weren't the gatherings of a small-time indy promotion; we were operating on a much grander stage. I can distinctly recall my initial experience setting up my ring for an NWA event. As the show's start time neared, Mr. Marquez approached me with a question that left me slightly embarrassed—where were the ring bell and the ring steps? Truth be told, I hadn't brought any with me.

This was a new requirement, a deviation from my past experiences in promotions that didn't use these elements from my ring setup. Mr. Marquez's reaction was a playful shake of the head, followed by a remark that stuck with me: "How the hell do you have a ring but no ring steps or a ring bell?" At that moment, I felt like I should have vanished into thin air. It was a lesson learned the hard way. Moving forward, I took diligent steps to ensure I always had the necessary ring steps and a functional ring bell on hand.

Further along in my wrestling journey, Impact Wrestling brought their show to San Antonio for "Lockdown" on March 10th, 2013. This event is still vividly remembered for the notable heel turn of Bubba Dudley and Aces & Eights. Alongside a couple of fellow students who were training with me at my home promotion, I had the opportunity to serve as gophers for the event. For those unfamiliar, being a gopher essentially meant being an assistant, running errands and fetching items as needed throughout the day.

This experience gave us an insider's view of the backstage atmosphere at Impact, and it was truly enlightening. The roster during that time was stacked with big names like AJ Styles, Hulk Hogan, Ric Flair, Jeff Hardy, and Sting, among others. The Alamodome was buzzing with excitement, packed to the brim that night. Being able to contribute behind the scenes and assist with the event was a fascinating and unforgettable experience.

Years later, I had the opportunity to be part of a pre-show match with Impact Wrestling through one of the promotions I was working for. It was a basic six-man tag featuring local talents, but the fact that we were on the same card as Impact Wrestling was incredibly exciting.

Working with Impact Wrestling showed me how well-organized and professionally run their shows are, even for the level they operate in. The level of production and attention to detail was impressive, and it was evident that they take their events seriously. It definitely felt like the big leagues compared to the indies. As someone accustomed to the independent wrestling scene, stepping into a TV or well-produced show environment was a whole different experience. I found myself feeling nervous while interacting with agents and producers, realizing that working on a well-produced show requires a different level of communication and precision.

Even though I was essentially an extra or enhancement talent for that particular match, being involved in such a high-quality production left a lasting impact on me. It gave me a glimpse of the level I aspired to reach in my wrestling journey, and it served as motivation to keep pushing forward and improving my skills.

Getting the chance to be an extra on a big-time production show is a tremendous opportunity for any indy wrestler. To make the most of such moments, always be prepared and ready for any role or task that comes your way. Ensure that your gear is in top condition and reflects your professionalism.

When you're in these productions, it's crucial to maintain a humble attitude and act with respect and courtesy towards everyone you encounter. Dress appropriately for the occasion and be proactive in offering help, even if it means assisting with setting up the ring or any other tasks required. During the event, take the opportunity to observe and learn from your surroundings. Be receptive to advice and guidance from those with more experience, and make a conscious effort to improve your skills and knowledge.

Remember, making a positive impression and conducting yourself in a professional manner can open doors for future opportunities. So, approach these experiences with a focus on learning, growing, and contributing positively to the overall production. Best of luck on your journey in the wrestling world!

Chapter 9
Road Trip Chronicles:
How I Accidentally Became 'Joey'

For the longest time, I simply wrestled under the name Specter – no other monikers or nicknames. However, everything changed during a wrestling road trip to California in 2005 with Rudy and some of the crew. We were set to wrestle for none other than the legendary Manny Fernandez, a true icon in the wrestling world. Manny's accolades from his NWA days, where he held tag team gold with Rick Rude, to his memorable battles in Southwest Championship Wrestling, were nothing short of awe-inspiring. The incident that made him infamous, involving a bloody encounter with the masked Invader in Puerto Rico on

May 11th, 1988, has become the stuff of wrestling legends.

The anticipation of wrestling for Manny Fernandez's promotion in California made the long road trip feel even more arduous. It was my first time venturing out to California, and the excitement was mixed with a bit of anxiety. As the hours stretched on, the journey seemed never-ending, and the hours on the road blurred together.

The road trip to Northern California took a toll on all of us. The cramped space in the vehicle, the endless stretches of highway, and the occasional rest stops made it feel like an eternity. But despite the fatigue and discomfort, there was a sense of fellowship among us. We shared stories, laughter, and the occasional wrestling trivia to keep our spirits high.

As we drove through different towns and landscapes, the excitement of the upcoming wrestling event kept us going. Each passing mile brought us closer to the opportunity of a lifetime – stepping into the ring for Manny Fernandez's promotion.

As the trip unfolded, Manny kept calling me "Joey" throughout the night, despite my real name being Eric. I found it both amusing and surreal that such an esteemed figure in wrestling history had mistaken my name. However, it wasn't until a pivotal moment during our conversation that I mustered the courage to correct him.

As Manny Fernandez continued to call me "Joey" throughout the day, I initially hesitated to correct him out of respect for his legendary status in the business. However, the more he referred to me as "Joey," the more the name started to resonate with me. It seemed to fit like a puzzle piece completing a picture, and I couldn't shake the feeling that "Joey Spector" was the right name for my wrestling persona.

In a break between matches, I mustered up the nerve to speak with Manny privately. "Manny, I appreciate the opportunity to be here, and I'm thrilled to wrestle for you. But my name is actually Eric, not Joey," I explained. This is a funny moment that whenever I run into him, we would bring up every time.

After some introspection, I decided to embrace the name "Joey Spector." It felt like a natural evolution of my character, and I knew it would help me stand out and leave a lasting impression on fans and fellow wrestlers alike. The name had a certain ring to it, and it gave my character a unique identity, which was essential in the competitive world of professional wrestling.

From that moment on, I introduced myself as "Joey Spector" to everyone I met, and it became my official wrestling name. Embracing this new identity allowed me to tap into a side of myself that I hadn't fully explored before – the cocky, cunning and relentless heel that would stop at nothing to get what he wanted.

Over time, "Joey Spector" became more than just a name; it became a persona that I could slip into effortlessly when stepping into the ring. The character took on a life of its own, and I found myself fully embodying the traits of a mean-spirited, rule-breaking antagonist. Indeed, it's fascinating how something as simple as a mispronunciation of a name can lead to a significant transformation in one's wrestling career. My journey as "Joey Spector" began with a mere misunderstanding, but it paved the way for a whole new persona that would define my wrestling path.

As time went on, Manny Fernandez's presence in Texas grew, and he became involved with various promotions in the area. I was fortunate enough to have the opportunity to work with him and receive his guidance at Rudy's wrestling school. Manny was the epitome of an old-school, no-nonsense veteran, and his tough and grizzled demeanor commanded respect.

I consider it a true honor to have been mentored, even if for a brief period, by someone as accomplished and respected as Manny Fernandez. He possessed an unparalleled wealth of knowledge and experience, and I soaked up every bit of wisdom he shared. Having mentored Rudy as well, Manny's influence extended to multiple generations of wrestlers, creating a sense of camaraderie and lineage among us all – branches of the same old tree.

During that particular journey to California, the atmosphere in the car got a bit heated, and tensions ran high among everyone. It felt like the tension was building, and it seemed like a fight could break out at any moment. Looking back, those intense moments are a testament to the passion and dedication we have for the wrestling business.

Despite the occasional shenanigans and heated tempers, road trips are an essential part of the wrestling experience. They bring wrestlers together, forging bonds that can last a lifetime. The shared experiences, both good and bad, create a unique sense of camaraderie that only fellow wrestlers can understand.

In the world of professional wrestling, road trips represent more than just transportation. They symbolize the journey we undertake, the challenges we face, and the growth we experience as performers. As we look back on those road trips, we may laugh at the shenanigans and remember the heated moments, but they all contribute to the richness and depth of our wrestling careers.

So, to all aspiring wrestlers out there, embrace the road trips, the moments of intensity, and the bonds that form along the way. They are all part of the incredible journey in the world of professional wrestling, shaping us into the performers we are meant to be.

Road trips are an integral part of the pro wrestling experience, providing valuable opportunities for learning, bonding, and sharing road stories with fellow wrestlers. While I may not go on as many road trips as I used to, the memories from those journeys are unforgettable. These trips are where you truly pay your dues, gaining experience and insights that shape you as a wrestler.

Going on road trips not only provides opportunities to wrestle in different places but also offers a chance to witness how veterans navigate the wrestling world. Hearing their road stories, sharing experiences, and picking up valuable tips all contribute to your growth as a performer.

A memorable road trip during the weekend of December 20th and 21st, 2002, led us to Bill Behren's NWA WildSide promotion in Georgia. This was the very place where AJ Styles kicked off his journey in the early 2000s, adding to its renowned reputation. I vividly recall watching videos of NWA WildSide at Prince Fontenot's house when I first started wrestling. So, you can imagine how surreal it felt to step into the ring and wrestle a few matches there. What made it even more thrilling was the fact that all matches were filmed for TV, usually lasting around 5 to 8 minutes. Learning the art of wrestling for television is a whole new ballgame, demanding precision, storytelling, and adaptability in a shorter time frame.

Wrestling on television brings a different set of challenges, especially when it comes to time constraints. Whether it's a live broadcast or taped show, you have to work within the allotted time, and there's little room for improvisation. The pressure is even greater when you're performing for someone like Mr. Behrens, with his connections to major wrestling promotions like WCW, TNA and WWE. You want to make a good impression and not mess up your chance to get your foot in the door.

NWA WildSide was a fun experience.

NWA WildSide was renowned for having some of the best wrestlers and workers of its time, making it a significant opportunity to showcase your talent. I vividly remember my first time there, wrestling for two back-to-back days. On the first night, I faced Tony Stradlin, another wrestler trained by Rudy Boy, and we had a decent 10-minute match. Stepping into the ring with Tony Stradlin was a defining moment in my wrestling journey. He was renowned as one of the best indy workers in the area, and his eventual WWE developmental deal spoke volumes about his talent. As we locked up, I felt the weight of the moment, but nerves soon gave way to the thrill of showcasing my skills in such a prestigious promotion like NWA WildSide.

Our match was a testament to the timeless art of chain wrestling and classic maneuvers, demonstrating the foundation of our craft. Tackles, drop-downs, and holds flowed effortlessly, building anticipation for the electrifying moments that followed. With the crowd engaged, we transitioned into a sequence of well-executed moves, and Tony cut me off, gaining the advantage.

His German suplex and other impactful maneuvers showed the finesse and hard-hitting nature of our craft. Even in this brief encounter, I felt the bond between two wrestlers, each striving to put on a memorable show for the enthusiastic crowd. It was a simple, yet satisfying match that left us both knowing we had made a positive impression.

The second night was a completely different experience. In that six-man tag team match, I found myself teaming up with Masada and another local wrestler from Rudy's against the formidable Fast Eddie, Kaos and his partner in crime, Scott Cage. Fast Eddie was an exceptional talent in the ring, and despite his legal blindness, he fearlessly executed death-defying maneuvers, earning his reputation as one of the best high-fliers in the state.

As I stepped into the ring, my nerves were on edge, especially considering the experienced and intense individuals I was sharing the squared circle with, especially Masada. While he could be intimidating at times, I knew that his passion for this business was unmatched, and we had forged a strong bond through years of working together.

The adrenaline was pumping as we clashed with Fast Eddie, Kaos and Scott Cage, the anticipation building with each move we exchanged. It was a fierce battle, and we all showcased our best skills and teamwork. The crowd roared with excitement as we took each other to the limit, displaying the heart and spirit of true warriors in the wrestling world. With the momentum shifting in our favor, our team of heels took control of the match. It was our moment to shine and unleash our calculated aggression on the faces. As the pressure built, I knew it was time to execute the spot I had planned, despite my nerves trying to hold me back.

In that crucial moment, doubts crept into my mind, questioning whether I was athletic enough to pull off the move as I envisioned it. The anxiety threatened to hinder my performance, but I took a deep breath, pushing those thoughts aside. I reminded myself that this was the time to step up, to embrace the challenge, and to give my all for the sake of the match and the fans who were eagerly watching.

Gathering my resolve, I trusted in the countless hours of training, the dedication I had poured into honing my craft, and the experience I had gained through countless battles in the ring. This was my opportunity to make an impact, to leave a lasting impression, and to show the world what I was capable of.

With determination fueling my actions, I went for the spot, pouring every ounce of energy into its execution. I attempted the high-flying move, but unfortunately, I slipped and ended up making a mistake. As the moment for the spot approached, I couldn't shake the nerves that had been building inside me. Despite my partners' encouragement and assurance that I had the athleticism to pull it off, self-doubt began to cloud my judgment. I considered suggesting a safer, less risky move, like a leg drop or an elbow drop, but they reminded me that this was NWA WildSide, and we needed to do something special to leave a lasting impression.

I took a deep breath and tried to muster up the confidence to go through with the spot. As we set up for it, my heart was pounding, and I felt a mix of excitement and fear. In that moment, I had to decide whether to trust in my abilities and take the risk or to let my doubts get the best of me.

I stepped onto my partner's back, ready to launch myself into the flipping senton. However, as I leaped off, something went awry. Maybe it was the nerves or the pressure of the moment, but I didn't fully commit to the flip. Instead, I landed awkwardly, and the move didn't have the impact I had hoped for. It was an epic fail, and I couldn't help but feel disappointed in myself. The story of my "botched" move became a talking point, but I had no intention to mess up; I was merely trying to do something impressive and stand out in front of the people running NWA WildSide.

While NWA WildSide, later known as NWA Anarchy, offered valuable opportunities and exposure, the financial rewards didn't always match the effort put in. I recall one particular instance when we received just $20 for the entire car after driving for over 12 hours. It was a stark reminder that passion and dedication to the craft often outshines the immediate financial gains in this business.

Promotions, especially those with strong reputations and historical significance, can provide a platform to showcase one's talent and potentially catch the attention of larger wrestling companies. However, these opportunities may not always come with a substantial paycheck. Wrestling on a regular basis for such promotions can be financially challenging, especially when travel expenses and time commitments are factored in.

I witnessed fellow wrestlers from Rudy's school who could make it work and attended weekly events at NWA WildSide or NWA Anarchy. However, circumstances varied, and I couldn't swing the same level of commitment at that time. It's essential for aspiring wrestlers to weigh their options and prioritize their goals. Some may prioritize frequent exposure and networking, while others may focus on balancing their passion for wrestling with other life commitments.

One of those standout trips was when I wrestled in Oklahoma for Ricky Morton's benefit show on February 26th, 2006. The event was dedicated to raising funds for something personal in Ricky's life, and it featured an exciting tag team tournament. Accompanied by Rudy and the crew, we embarked on a journey filled with legends of the wrestling world.

The roster for Ricky Morton's benefit show read like a who's who of old school wrestling with iconic names such as Cowboy Bill Watts, Tom Jones, Ricky Morton himself, and even Dr. Death Steve Williams. These individuals are true legends, and it was an absolute honor to be in their presence and share the ring with them.

During the trip, I found myself playfully teasing and ribbing Rudy, which eventually led to some hilarious antics between us. Our playful banter escalated into a shoot wrestling match in the hotel, resulting in us ending up outside the room in the landscaping. He may or may not have tried to shove some of the landscaping rocks in my butt-crack for annoying him all trip. It was all in good fun, and moments like these epitomize the lighter side of wrestling. These shenanigans create memories that will be cherished for a lifetime, bonding wrestlers together in a unique way.

Overall, the show was an amazing experience and I loved the old school feel of being around the old timers. For those unfamiliar with these legendary wrestlers, I highly recommend using Google to search them up and learn about their remarkable contributions to the wrestling world. Being in the company of such icons added to the significance of the road trip and made it an experience I'll always treasure. Wrestling isn't just about in-ring action; it's also about the friendships, and the unforgettable moments that happen along the way, making it a truly unique and special journey for every wrestler.

One incident that remains vivid in my memory occurred as I was leaving a gas station in Mississippi around February 2006. As I drove, I suddenly heard a loud thud in the back of the van. When I got out to investigate, I was shocked to find a homeless guy lying on the ground, knocked out. It turned out that I had accidentally reversed into him as he was walking right behind the van. It was such a bizarre and unexpected situation that I couldn't help but burst into laughter, though I was relieved to see that he was alright. He seemed to be quite intoxicated, so I helped him up, moved him to a safe spot and then we continued on our way.

Of course, there are many other hilarious and crazy stories from wrestling road trips, but to protect everyone's privacy and avoid any potential trouble, I'd rather keep those memories to myself. That's one of the best things about having wrestling memories—they become cherished and often humorous anecdotes that are shared among wrestlers like a secret language, forming a bond that only those who've experienced it can truly understand.

In the world of wrestling, ribbing and pranks are not uncommon, and they add to the lightheartedness of the journey. These moments create a unique tapestry of memories that unite wrestlers and become part of the fabric of the wrestling world. While some stories will remain a treasured part of our own experiences, it's these shared experiences and funny memories that make the wrestling community truly special.

Throughout my journey, I've had the incredible opportunity to wrestle in a diverse array of wrestling promotions spanning various states, from the heart of Louisiana to the excitement of California and beyond. It's fascinating to witness how wrestling differs in each region, showcasing unique styles and passionate fan bases that make every event a truly distinct experience.

Despite these regional variations, there's a beautiful thread of continuity in the teachings and traditions passed down in the wrestling world. Time-honored principles and techniques, imparted by seasoned veterans and mentors, serve as the backbone of this business. These shared values form a solid foundation that unites wrestlers regardless of where they come from or where they perform.

Embracing the chance to wrestle in new territories, especially when guided by experienced promoters or respected veterans, can be an enlightening experience. These road trips provide not just physical mileage but also an opportunity for personal growth. As you navigate unfamiliar environments, learn from different perspectives, and bond with fellow wrestlers, you gain invaluable insights that shape your own journey in this captivating industry.

Road trip to Kansas with the boys (Behind me Danny & Scott)

If ever the door opens to venture out of town and take part in a promotion run by an old-timer or seasoned figure, seize that moment. Such experiences offer a chance to enhance your skills, expand your network, and foster unforgettable memories. Embracing road trips with enthusiasm enriches your wrestling career, enriching you with a tapestry of encounters, friendships, and knowledge that truly makes this business a remarkable adventure. So, embrace the road, relish the opportunities, and let each mile fuel your passion for the world of professional wrestling.

Now I don't want to exactly be a buzzkill and tell you guys a bad road trip story, but this is one that I absolutely have to share because it was a life changing event for me that I will never forget.

I've got a chilling story to share, stemming from a road trip I took with my father on February 18th, 2007. We were en route to the Dallas-Fort Worth area for a wrestling event—the Konnan benefit show. It was organized to raise funds for Konnan from WCW and in Impact Wrestling, who was dealing with some medical issues at the time. The event had gone well, and I was making the long drive back home, which was about a 5-hour journey.

As I was on the road, heading towards Austin, Texas, a sudden and unexpected danger emerged. Out of nowhere, I noticed a car stopped right in the middle of the highway. It happened so fast that I couldn't react in time, and I ended up rear-ending the car at full speed, around 70 miles an hour. The impact was jarring and terrifying.

The experience was nothing short of a nightmare. The initial shock was followed by a flood of adrenaline and the realization of what had just occurred. I was fortunate enough to have my seat belt on, which likely saved me from severe injuries. However, the car was in bad shape, and the scene was chaotic. My father and I were both shaken but thankfully not seriously hurt.

I can vividly recall the terrifying moments when everything turned chaotic. The sound of shattering glass filled the air, accompanied by the sensation of my dashboard and steering wheel pressing against me with an overwhelming force. The airbag deployed with a jolt that sent me into a daze, momentarily knocking me out. Amid the confusion, my father's anguished cries pierced through the chaos, a stark reminder that we were in grave danger.

As the scene unfolded, the consequences of the crash became painfully evident. The other car, the one we had collided with, was struck by an 18-wheeler with an unforgiving force. The collision sent that car hurtling through the air, a jaw-dropping sight that underscored the magnitude of the disaster.

After the impact, I found myself trapped in the driver's seat of my car. Adrenaline surged through me as I fought to free myself from the confines of the wreckage. In a haze of urgency, I managed to extricate myself from the mangled metal, my heart pounding in my chest. But my father was in a different situation. Pain gripped him, and he was unable to move. It was a distressing scene, one that made me acutely aware of the fragility of life and the suddenness with which everything can change.

Thankfully, EMTs and ambulances arrived within five minutes. They rushed the driver of the other car to the hospital, and my dad, due to his age, was taken as well. I waited at a nearby gas station for someone to come pick me up, my anxiety growing as I wondered about my dad's condition. As it turned out, the other car's driver was drunk and clearly shouldn't have been on the road. Learning this angered me. It was frustrating to think that someone's irresponsible actions put both our lives in danger. It was a stark reminder of how individual choices can impact others in life-altering ways.

That incident left deep emotional scars. Whenever I'm driving and see cars brake suddenly, panic kicks in. Tailgating cars or being on the road for too long triggers anxiety. I can't help but think about what might have happened if my car had swerved into the middle lane instead of veering onto the grass. The "what ifs" haunt me. Yet, despite the fear and trauma, one thing remains clear: luck was on my side that evening. It's like God was watching out for me. The accident served as a jarring reminder of life's fragility and the unpredictability of driving. The experience shook me to my core, but it also deepened my gratitude for the time I have with my loved ones. It was a terrifying event that I hope never recurs, but it's made me more cautious and vigilant whenever I'm on the road.

Reflecting on that harrowing experience, it's impossible not to feel a sense of profound gratitude. The series of events that led to the crash could easily have played out differently. If fate had led us to switch places with the occupants of the other car, the outcome could have been tragically different.

Chapter 10
From Sober to Supershot:
How I Drank My Way to My Gimmick

In the world of professional wrestling, every aspiring wrestler enters with a cool character, a gimmick, in mind that they can't wait to bring to life in the ring. I was no exception. When I first stepped into the squared circle, I had a vivid vision of becoming a high-flying hero, donning a wrestling mask and wowing the crowd with daring acrobatics. It seemed like the perfect persona for me, and I was eager to make it a reality.

However, as I immersed myself in the world of wrestling and gained experience, I soon realized that the path to finding the right character wasn't as straightforward as I thought. Despite my enthusiasm for the high-flying hero persona, the reality was far from my initial expectations. I discovered that the character I envisioned wasn't truly connecting with the audience or bringing out the best in me as a performer.

It was a pivotal moment in my wrestling journey when I decided to reassess my character and explore new possibilities. This process of self-discovery opened my eyes to the importance of allowing a character to evolve organically, rather than forcing it to fit a predetermined mold. As I stepped back from my original gimmick, I began to explore different aspects of my personality, wrestling style, and interactions with the audience.

During my early days, I donned a black Karate outfit with face paint, dubbing myself "The Specter." But soon, I felt the urge to transform my character and opted for a wrestling mask adorned with a skull, inspired by the likes of Chris Kanyon's "Mortis" persona from WCW. However, despite the excitement of my new gimmick, the mask didn't feel like the right fit, and I wore it only once.

After shedding the wrestling mask and being known simply as "Specter," I found myself in a bit of a wrestling identity crisis. The character lacked a defined identity, and I struggled to connect with the audience. It became evident that portraying a dark, evil persona as a 5'6" tall and 100 lb wrestler wasn't entirely convincing. The reality set in that I needed a character that would be more believable and relatable to the fans.

Acknowledging this reality, I made a significant decision to step away from the dark persona and embraced the path of a generic wrestler. I became adaptable, transforming my role based on the dynamics of the match and the crowd's response. Depending on the night and the opponent, I could seamlessly transition between a heel or a face, adapting my demeanor and actions accordingly.

Being generic isn't good in this business though. I yearned for a character that could truly stand out, something more than just a change of gear. During this period, a significant shift happened in my journey. On July 2nd, 2004, I joined forces with Darin Childs to create the Rock and Roll Nightmares tag team, marking a pivotal moment. This partnership marked the emergence of my first genuine gimmick, breathing new life into my wrestling career.

With the Rock and Roll Nightmares, I found a character that had depth and personality, allowing me to showcase a different side of myself. We embodied the spirit of rebellious rock stars, captivating the audience with our charisma and showmanship. It was a liberating experience to have a distinct gimmick that resonated with the fans, and our chemistry as a tag team brought a whole new level of excitement to my wrestling journey.

As I began wrestling for multiple companies, I noticed a fascinating pattern emerge - at each place, I found myself adopting various gimmicks and personas. However, it wasn't until I gained momentum as a solid baby face that things truly started to click for me. The wrestling world embraced me as an underdog type, and I looked to iconic figures like Sean Waltman, the 1-2-3 kid, for inspiration.

In no time, I became known as the "Upset Kid," a moniker that perfectly captured my knack for achieving upset victories at the promotion. It seemed like the fans were rooting for me, and I fed off their energy. Being the underdog was invigorating; it motivated me to push harder and prove myself in every match I stepped into.

As the Upset Kid, I had the privilege of experiencing some of the most memorable moments of my career. The thrill of turning the tide against more formidable opponents and securing surprising wins made each victory even sweeter. The fans' support and the buzz surrounding my matches propelled me to new heights, solidifying my status as a crowd favorite.

The Upset Kid" Joey Spector

Indeed, that period as the Upset Kid was undoubtedly one of the most cherished moments in my wrestling journey. The overwhelming love and support from the fans were something I'll never forget. But as time passed, I noticed a curious trend that seems to be ingrained in wrestling fandom - a fickleness that often accompanies prolonged periods of being a beloved baby face. It seemed that the longer I portrayed the lovable underdog, the more the fans yearned for something different, leading to a slow shift in their sentiments.

In an effort to keep things fresh and exciting, I delved into experimenting with various gimmicks, hoping to find that one elusive persona that would truly resonate with the audience. From donning flashy '80s attire to trying out eyeliner, I left no stone unturned in my quest for the perfect character. However, despite my best efforts, none of these attempts seemed to strike a lasting chord with the fans.

As they say, you "throw shit at the wall and see what sticks", and that's precisely what I did. But for a while, it felt like nothing was sticking. It was a challenging phase of my career where I grappled with finding my true identity in the wrestling world. Yet, despite the uncertainties, I refused to lose hope. Every setback served as a valuable lesson, and I was determined to use those experiences to mold myself into a more refined and captivating performer.

In the world of professional wrestling, evolution is a constant companion. As a wrestler, one must adapt to the changing tides, constantly refining and redefining their character to stay relevant and keep the fans engaged. While the search for my ideal gimmick may have been a roller-coaster of ups and downs, it was also a journey of self-discovery and growth.

Ultimately, I learned that the key to success in this industry lies in embracing one's authenticity and showcasing the genuine passion and dedication that fuels the love for wrestling. It's not just about finding the perfect gimmick; it's about being true to oneself and allowing the fans to connect with the real person behind the character.

On November 4th, 2006, I became a member of a comedy stable named the Hard Bodies, along with Andy Dalton and JT Lamotta. Being part of the Hard Bodies stable was a unique and memorable chapter in my wrestling career. As an Ambiguously Gay Trio portraying Gym Rats, we embraced our distinct characters and had a blast playing up the antics in the ring. Despite not fitting the conventional mold of physically fit gym enthusiasts, our commitment to the roles and our solid in-ring skills garnered us significant heel heat.

Our chemistry as a stable was undeniable, and that translated into some exceptional matches against some of the most beloved baby faces in South Texas at the time. The wrestling scene in the region was thriving, and we found ourselves in the thick of it, engaging in hard-fought battles and unforgettable feuds.

As heels, we reveled in pushing the boundaries of fan reactions, stirring emotions, and riling up the crowd. Every time we stepped into the ring, we aimed to leave a lasting impression on both our opponents and the audience. Our technical prowess and well-coordinated performances brought the best out of our opponents, leading to thrilling encounters that had fans on the edge of their seats.

When I debuted as part of the Hardbodies

A significant moment in my wrestling journey unfolded unexpectedly at a New Year's Eve party in 2010. I was among friends, including my wrestling companions Josh Long and Ruben Steele, who happened to be playing the role of bartender for the night. It was during this revelry that the idea for my iconic gimmick, the "Supershot," was born.

Feeling adventurous and perhaps a bit foolish, I playfully challenged Ruben to concoct a drink with every single type of alcohol available at the party, and without hesitation, he expertly mixed it together. Little did I know that this daring choice would shape my wrestling persona forever.

Downing the concoction, I was dubbed the "Supershot" – a moniker that seemed amusing and lighthearted at the time. In my carefree spirit, I made the mistake of taking a second one, and from there, the night became a hazy blur of laughter and partying.

The next day, I woke up with the hangover of a lifetime, but what I didn't realize was that the nickname "Supershot" had taken root, I decided to embrace the persona, molding it into the perfect blend of my mischievous, rule-breaking nature and my knack for getting under the skin of my opponents and the audience. The "Supershot" became my alter ego, a character that embodied the chip on my shoulder for the last decade of my career.

The journey to finding the perfect gimmick and fully embracing the "Supershot" character was a defining moment in my wrestling career. It was around 2010 when I realized that trying to please everyone and seeking approval was not the way to go. Instead, I needed to focus on crafting matches that brought out raw emotions and delivered captivating storytelling.

I embraced the role of a villain, immersing myself in the persona that I knew would draw the audience's ire. I became the embodiment of everything people love to hate—a relentless, classless heel who would stop at nothing to claim victory. I wasn't afraid to bend the rules, to cheat and manipulate my way to success, and I felt no shame in doing so.

In the ring, I played the part of an unapologetic aggressor, willing to cross any line to secure a win. I didn't hold back, delivering forceful chops and pulling opponents by their hair without a second thought. My actions were calculated to incite the crowd, to provoke their anger and disdain. On the mic, I abandoned all filters, spewing forth cutting insults and taunts that riled up the audience like never before. I relished in being insufferable, relaying my contempt for anyone and everyone who dared to challenge me.

The debut of my "Supershot" persona in 2010.

Being the antagonist brought out a side of me that was both exhilarating and challenging. It demanded a level of commitment and fearlessness to delve into the darker aspects of my character. As a performer, I had to find the balance between staying true to the character's essence and ensuring the audience knew it was all part of the show.

Stepping into the role of a ruthless, hated heel allowed me to explore a different dimension of wrestling, tapping into emotions and reactions that are unique to this kind of character. It was a chance to master the art of provoking a response from the audience, even if it meant pushing the boundaries of what was acceptable.

With the birth of the "Supershot" gimmick, I tapped into a different side of my personality, embracing a cocky, chauvinistic, and women-hating chicken heel persona. It was a complete departure from the previous iterations of my character, and for the first time, I felt like I had found my true wrestling identity.

This transformation allowed me to delve deeper into my performances, bringing a level of authenticity to the character that resonated with the audience. As Supershot, I reveled in eliciting reactions from the crowd, making them hate me with every fiber of their being. It was liberating to fully embrace the heel side of me and use it to drive the story lines forward.

If you're an aspiring wrestler, remember not to lose hope and always pay attention to the crowd's reactions. In my own journey, I discovered that my hairy legs elicited a response from the audience, leading to "shave your legs" chants. Instead of ignoring it, I embraced this natural heat and decided to showcase my hairy legs in my gear.

It's essential to recognize that any reaction from the crowd, no matter how seemingly insignificant, can be valuable in shaping your character. Whether it's something as simple as hairy legs, a distinctive feature, or a unique personality trait, embrace it fully and incorporate it into your persona. These natural reactions can set you apart and make your character more authentic and relatable.

In the world of wrestling, the worst thing that can happen is indifference from the audience. So, if you're receiving any form of reaction, consider it a positive sign that you're making an impact. Embrace what makes you stand out, whether it's cheers or boos, as long as it draws a response from the crowd. Personalize your character and use those natural reactions to your advantage, building a connection with the audience that leaves a lasting impression.

Remember, your journey as a wrestler is about self-discovery and evolution. Don't shy away from what makes you unique, no matter how unconventional it may seem. Instead, use these aspects to create a captivating and memorable persona. Keep an open mind, be confident in who you are, and always strive to evoke emotions and entertain the fans, as they are the heartbeat of professional wrestling.

In the world of professional wrestling, connecting with the crowd is paramount. Fans love to be engaged and participate in the experience, even if it means chanting something unexpected or irregular. Wrestlers should recognize that these spontaneous reactions from the crowd can be a powerful tool in building their character and connecting with the audience on a deeper level.

Adaptability is a key attribute for any successful wrestler. Instead of shying away from anything the crowd might chant, use it as a stepping stone to create an engaging story line or persona around it. By wholeheartedly embracing the chant, you can turn it into something unique and memorable, allowing the audience to feel more invested in your character.

Indeed, finding the right gimmick or character in wrestling is a journey unique to each individual, including myself. There's no one-size-fits-all formula for success in this business. The key is to let it happen naturally and be open to trying different approaches until something clicks.

Throughout my career, I've been asked to portray various characters and perform tasks that I may not have initially been comfortable with. Some of it may have seemed silly or even ridiculous, but I've learned that versatility and adaptability are crucial traits in the world of wrestling. As an aspiring wrestler, you may find yourself in similar situations where you're asked to take on roles that challenge your comfort zone.

In my old-school training, I was taught to put my ego aside, focus on getting paid, and do what was required of me during the show. Each promotion may have different creative visions, and being willing to embrace different characters or story lines can open doors to more opportunities in the wrestling industry.

Even if something seems odd or not in line with your original vision, it's essential to remember that wrestling is a business, and sometimes you have to make certain compromises for the greater good of your career. Embracing diverse experiences and characters can help you grow as a performer and gain valuable exposure to various wrestling styles and audiences.

In the ever-evolving world of wrestling, your character and role can change rapidly. It's essential to live in the moment and embrace each opportunity to get over with the audience. Throughout my wrestling journey, there was one person who played a pivotal role in helping me unleash my inner showman and take my heel persona to the next level: Shawn Hernandez, also known as Super-Mex.

While he might not seek recognition, I can't help but express my gratitude for the significant impact Shawn had on my career. With his guidance and insight, we explored the potential I had in eliciting genuine reactions from the crowd, particularly as a compelling heel. Embracing my ability to draw the audience's ire effortlessly opened new doors for me as a performer.

Shawn's mentorship and the candid discussions we had allowed me to refine my skills and refine my character's nuances. He encouraged me to break boundaries and explore different aspects of my persona, paving the way for my growth as a wrestler and entertainer. It was an invaluable partnership that truly pushed me to new heights.

Me and Shawn cutting up in the ring after a match.

In the ever-changing landscape of professional wrestling, having mentors like Shawn Hernandez can be a game-changer. Their experience and support not only shape your on-screen character but also nurture your growth as an individual within the business. I will always appreciate his willingness to share his knowledge and selflessly help me reach new levels of success.

Throughout the years, Shawn Hernandez offered a wealth of valuable suggestions and guidance that significantly shaped my wrestling journey. Our relationship evolved into a mutual respect where we understood each other's preferences and strengths when it came to booking for the promotions I wrestled for. Once I grasped what he liked and embraced his advice, it proved to be golden for my career.

Back in my teenage years, I must admit I was a bit headstrong and, at times, self-sabotaged my potential without even realizing it. Despite my talent, I lacked the perfect formula to truly get over with the crowd. Shawn would occasionally express frustration, recognizing the untapped potential within me.

However, as time went on, I had a profound "aha" moment. It took nearly a decade into my wrestling career, but I finally understood the essence of my character and how to portray it effectively. It was a turning point where I shed the ego and embraced the wisdom of those who had walked the path before me, including Shawn.

Once I aligned myself with his expertise and embraced his guidance, my character began to flourish. The chemistry we developed in understanding each other's vision for my character led to outstanding performances inside the ring and exceptional crowd reactions.

Looking back, I can't help but appreciate the journey that brought me to this realization. Wrestling is not just about physical prowess; it's an intricate dance of storytelling, psychology, and connecting with the audience. I am forever grateful for Shawn Hernandez's impact on my career, helping me unlock the full potential of my character and paving the way for unforgettable moments in the squared circle.

Shawn and I share a history of numerous matches over the years, and we've also joined forces as a tag team, securing championship titles in various promotions. However, there's one particular match that stands out vividly in my memory. This happened over Easter weekend in 2011, adding an unexpected twist to our meeting. As the match progressed, our routine unfolded – Shawn dishing out his signature chops, and me reacting accordingly.

Then came the unexpected moment that etched itself into my mind. Positioned at ringside, I found myself tossed out of the ring, creating a brief pause in the action. To my astonishment, there, right by the ring, were two Easter baskets, as if placed there by cosmic happenstance. The spontaneity of the situation struck a chord, and it was as if the wrestling gods were offering a quirky diversion from the norm.

In a whimsical turn, Shawn seized both baskets, transforming them into unorthodox weapons. The colorful cascarones within, when smashed against my head, exploded in a cascade of confetti, showering the area with vibrant fragments. The visual spectacle created by this impromptu act injected an element of surprise and amusement, adding a unique dimension to our match.

Reflecting on our journey together, Shawn remains one of the select few individuals with whom I share an unparalleled chemistry in the ring. Our synergy is so finely tuned that I could execute moves almost instinctively, even if I were to close my eyes. Our encounters stand as a testament to the remarkable rapport we've developed over time, allowing us to craft engaging and memorable moments like the Easter basket incident that continue to resonate with fans and wrestling enthusiasts.

Hernandez's impact on my wrestling career was nothing short of transformative, and I am forever grateful for his mentorship and guidance. He possesses an innate understanding of the craft, and his willingness to lend a helping hand was a rare gem in the business.

With his support and expertise, I was able to evolve into the Supershot, reaching heights I never thought possible. His keen eye for storytelling and psychology helped me unlock the true essence of my character, allowing me to connect with the audience like never before.

So, here's a heartfelt shout-out to Shawn for being a pivotal force in my journey. Your belief in my potential and the opportunities you provided helped me become a top-notch heel in the fiercely competitive wrestling scene of South Texas.

Thank you, Shawn, for being a guiding light and helping me become the wrestler I am today. Your impact will resonate throughout my entire career, and I cherish every moment we shared in the ring. "Es Hot Today!"

Chapter 11
Tales of Wrestling Pranks and Bathroom Shenanigans

In the world of pro wrestling, there's an unspoken code called kayfabe that emphasizes the importance of keeping certain stories and backstage antics private, out of respect for the business and the individuals involved. While I have a treasure trove of funny ribs, pranks, and memorable experiences, I understand the significance of maintaining that sense of camaraderie and trust among fellow wrestlers.

As much as I'd love to provide you with all the humorous and entertaining moments, I choose to respect the privacy and dignity of my peers. It's a delicate balance between sharing the joy of wrestling and preserving the mystique that captivates fans and performers alike.

The wrestling fraternity is a close-knit community, and the trust and respect shared among its members are invaluable. By cherishing these stories within our circles, we reinforce the bond that unites us as wrestlers and professionals. It's a testament to the passion we have for this business, and it ensures that the magic of pro wrestling endures for both performers and fans. While I may not be able to divulge all the uproarious anecdotes, I can assure you that the world of pro wrestling is brimming with laughter and unforgettable moments.

I've come to understand and appreciate the time-honored tradition of ribs and pranks within the business. It's a way of bonding with my fellow wrestlers and sharing moments of laughter and comradery. However, I always approach these pranks with a sense of respect and consideration for others.

I firmly believe in the principle of treating others as I would like to be treated. If I decide to play a rib on someone, I am fully prepared to receive an equal measure of revenge in return. It's all part of the fun and the close-knit community we share.

When engaging in ribs, I make sure they are done in good taste and meant to bring smiles rather than discomfort. The objective is to create a positive atmosphere and cherish the memories we make together. If at any point a rib goes beyond someone's comfort zone or becomes too much, I'm quick to stop and apologize. Respect for my colleagues' boundaries is of utmost importance to me.

While some may misconstrue ribs as hazing or bullying, I firmly disagree. In the right context and with mutual consent, they can be a lighthearted expression of brotherhood and friendship. It's almost a rite of passage to be ribbed; it's about building connections and lasting memories within the wrestling community.

It's always fun to reminisce about the good old ribbing days in wrestling. Back when I started at Rudy Boys in 2002, we had this guy named Mark, and for some reason, he left his car at the wrestling school. Well, you can imagine what happened next – it was just too tempting to resist pulling a little prank on him.

Me and another student at the school decided we would do the classic TP of the car prank to Mark.

My partner-in-crime and I decided to go ahead with the TP-ing, thinking it would be a good laugh. Surprisingly, Mark never mentioned anything about the prank or his car being messed with, so we thought we got away with it. Little did we know, karma had a funny way of striking back.

One day, while my accomplice and I were practicing a full wrestling match in the ring, Rudy suddenly yelled, "Now go!" Confused, we looked around and saw everyone outside the ring rolling the canvas up like we were being wrapped into burritos. And that's not all – someone produced a full-size roll of Saran Wrap and started wrapping it around our legs!

Mark came up with a devious plan and pulled out a bottle of Nair hair removal. He, along with some accomplices, carefully applied it to both of our eyebrows, and we had to wait the excruciating 3 minutes for the Nair to take effect. Once they wiped it off, to our shock and amusement, we were both eyebrowless! I couldn't help but burst into laughter, even though I knew this revenge rib would have some consequences.

Unfortunately, the timing couldn't have been worse; my high school graduation was just around the corner, less than a week away. Walking the stage without eyebrows wasn't something I had anticipated. But you know what they say, the show must go on! During my last week at school, I turned to my girlfriend for help. She sweetly took on the task of drawing my eyebrows back on, and she did an impressive job, saving the day and ensuring I could face my graduation with confidence or so I thought.

My high school friend Edwin took the prank to a whole new level by running up to me and smearing my drawn-on eyebrows. It was a messy sight, and I couldn't even clean it up properly. Those eyebrows took forever to grow back, and I learned the hard way that wrestling ribs could have some lasting consequences.

As time passed, I discovered that Mark was the mastermind behind the whole thing, and he had paid off the entire wrestling school to be part of this elaborate revenge rib. It was quite the eye-opener for me and definitely a memorable initiation into the world of wrestling pranks. It was all in good fun, though, and looking back, I can't help but laugh at how I got my first receipt in the wrestling business.

In the previous chapter, I touched upon my tag team partnership with Darin Childs. One particular memory stands out before a Rudy Boy's show. We were in the ring warming up alongside other roster members, and Rudy Russo was also there, rolling around. In a spur-of-the-moment challenge, I proposed a shoot-style mat wrestling match with Russo. He easily dispatched me in no time. Not one to back down, I called for a rematch. And then another. And another. The scenario repeated, with me getting taken down swiftly each time.

In fact, I mustered up the courage for a rematch six times in a row. It became a running joke among us that Rudy Russo had managed to legitimately pin me multiple times, leaving him visibly out of breath by the end. Little did he know, it was all a playful rib. Our intention was to tire him out before his scheduled handicap match against us later in the show. It was a lighthearted prank that became a cherished memory among us. As 20 years went by, Russo finally cracked the code of our elaborate rib.

From 2007 to 2008, I had the opportunity to wrestle for Xtreme Championship Wrestling (XCW), a company in Denton, Texas. It was a weekly TV taping wrestling show that drew quite the rowdy crowd, especially since it allowed BYOB for the audience and was located near a college. Spending weekends there for two years created strong bonds among the boys, and with that came some unforgettable pranks. Now, I must warn you that the following story involves potty humor, so if that's not your thing, you might want to skip the next few paragraphs.

For a little while, there was a wrestler from a different country, possibly Denmark, staying at the apartment of two of the boys, Danny and Scott. After the wrestler left, an unusual conversation arose, suggesting that they suspected him of leaving feces in their bathtub. Weeks went by, and coincidentally, it happened to be Scott's birthday. He decided to host a house party at their apartment. On the way there, one of my buddies who was riding with me challenged me, claiming I didn't have the nerve to take a dump in Scott's bathtub and blame it on the wrestler from Denmark.

Facing challenges and not backing down is part of the wrestling brotherhood, and I was no exception. Embracing the memories and shenanigans with my boys, I took on the challenge with gusto, knowing that refusing to back down would spare me from a rib for lacking the guts. I was fully aware that a receipt would be coming my way, and I welcomed it, understanding that it's all in good fun and part of the traditions we shared in the wrestling world.

Me and Scott McKenzie

During the night, as everyone was enjoying themselves with food and drinks, I saw the perfect opportunity for some epic humor, especially since Scott probably forgot he had told us that story. When it was time to leave, I couldn't resist the chance to pull the prank. Sneaking into the bathroom, I carefully left one little turd in the bathtub and then quietly made my exit, saying my goodbyes to everyone. We were already on the road for about an hour when I received a phone call from Scott, exclaiming, "What is this? There's shit in my bathtub!"

As I played innocent, I couldn't shake the feeling that someone had snitched on me. Sure enough, after a couple of weeks, the inevitable receipt arrived. For those unfamiliar with wrestling terms, a receipt is when someone gets back at you for a prank. I knew it was coming, but the timing caught me off guard. One day, just when I least expected it, I finished my match and returned to my bag. To my surprise, it was filled to the brim with kitty litter, emitting a foul smell and covering all my clothes. It was a clever and well-executed prank that I couldn't help but laugh about. Embracing the traditions of the wrestling world, I no-sold it, showing no reaction, and even wore the same clothes to the bar later that evening, letting the fun and laughter continue.

Throughout my wrestling journey, I've witnessed some fantastic pranks, and I've come to realize that simplicity often yields the best results. There was a mysterious figure known as the "Unidentified Padlock Bandit" who roamed from locker room to locker room, playfully padlocking people's wrestling bags to chairs and even water jugs. Imagine the hassle it created when wrestlers had to figure out how to remove a padlock without knowing the combination or having a key! It may have been a straightforward prank, but its effectiveness in bringing laughter among the wrestlers was truly remarkable.

One unforgettable moment backstage was when someone's brand new wrestling boots ended up super glued to a table. The prank left them struggling to pull their boots off the table, creating a hilarious and memorable situation. Another classic trick we often pulled on each other during meals was sneaking salt into each other's drinks when they left them unattended. The look of surprise on their faces when they took a sip with that unexpected salty twist always brought us all to tears of laughter.

The mattress trick was a classic prank we loved to play on each other during hotel stays. It involved pre-arranging the box spring and top mattress of a colleague's bed, switching their positions so that the box spring ended up on top. We would carefully make the bed to look normal, and when they went to lay down, they'd find themselves uncomfortably resting on the hard surface of the box spring. The look of confusion and surprise on their face was always worth the effort we put into setting up this mischievous trick.

To take the mattress trick to the next level, we'd make it a friendly challenge. I'd showcase a cool trick on my bed, saying, "Hey, I bet you can't top this!" Naturally, they'd be tempted to show off their skills and accept the challenge. Little did they know that we had switched their box spring with the mattress. As they leaped onto their bed with confidence, expecting to perform the trick, they'd land on the unsuspecting hard box spring!

Wrestling at South Padre Island for Carmine Despirito was always a memorable experience, and one particular night stands out vividly in my mind. After the wrestling show on February 15th, 2009, I chose to unwind and enjoy some drinks with my fellow wrestlers. As the night progressed, the drinks kept flowing, and before I knew it, I was completely hammered. Originally, I planned to head back home after the show since I had work the next evening, but the excitement and camaraderie of the moment got the better of me.

Realizing that I was in no condition to drive, I knew I had to crash at the hotel for the night. As I stumbled my way to our shared room, I was looking forward to a comfortable night's sleep. However, as I collapsed onto the bed, I was met with a rude awakening - or should I say, a rude landing! Instead of the expected plush mattress, I landed right on a box spring bed. My intoxicated state made it nearly impossible for me to switch the box spring with the top mattress, so I ended up in a humorous yet uncomfortable predicament - sandwiched between both the box spring and the top mattress.

While it may not have been the most restful night of sleep, it certainly became a legendary ribbing story among us wrestlers. My buddies couldn't help but burst into laughter as I recounted my misadventure the next morning. They cheekily reminded me that the box spring trick had been perfectly executed, and they were impressed with my improvised solution to sleep between the layers.

One of the most memorable ribs in my wrestling journey revolves around our beloved security guards who had been with us for years, practically becoming part of our wrestling family. As time passed, their relationship with the wrestlers grew, and they truly became "some of the boys."

Let me tell you about one of the most unforgettable pranks in wrestling history, known as the "Masked Humper." Now, I wasn't the mastermind behind this hilarious trick, but I found myself becoming an accomplice when I learned about it. This story takes place at a promotion that shall remain nameless, where the crew decided to orchestrate this rib on the unsuspecting security guard during every show.

The plan was simple yet cunning: at some point during each event, usually around intermission when the security guard was occupied away from ringside, a masked individual dressed in nothing but their underwear would stealthily make their way to the wrestling ring. The daring act? Well, they would engage in some playful humping, either targeting the referee or one of the wrestlers. The spectacle was equal parts shocking and sidesplitting, leaving everyone in stitches.

As part of the inside circle, we were all in on the prank, anticipating the opportune moment to strike. Once the Masked Humper made their move, we seized the perfect chance to play along. In the most dramatic fashion, we rushed up to the security guard, feigning panic, and urgently informed them about the mysterious intruder in the wrestling ring. Obliging to their duty, the guard would quickly spring into action, hurrying to the ring to apprehend the "culprit."

What made the prank even more amusing was the Masked Humper's uncanny ability to make a swift and undetected escape. Before the security guard could lay eyes on the mischievous prankster, they had already vanished into thin air, leaving everyone amazed at their clever getaway.

The Masked Humper escapades became an ongoing delight, and as time went on, I was unwittingly drawn into the scheme. Once I learned about the secret behind the masked figure, it sparked a fun little game to outsmart the security guard every show and keep the ribbing alive. It became a backstage tradition, adding a layer of excitement to the already thrilling wrestling experience. The thrill of anticipation grew stronger as we strategized and plotted, trying to figure out new and inventive ways to distract the security guard. It became a playful challenge to see who could successfully divert their attention while the Masked Humper prepared to strike.

However, one fateful day, during the hustle and bustle of show preparation, we unintentionally forgot to carry out the distraction plan. Unbeknownst to us, the security guard was fully alert and primed, ready to catch the mischievous jester red-handed. As the Masked Humper made their characteristic dash toward the ring, the security guard was lightning fast, nabbing them in a reverse choke hold before they could escape.

A moment of confusion and panic ensued, with the security guard genuinely believing they had apprehended a genuine intruder. His firm grip and fierce determination to hold onto his "prize" left us scrambling to explain the situation, desperate to defuse the situation before it escalated further. "Hey, hey, it's all good! It's all good! It's just a prank!" we urgently pleaded as we tried to pry the guard off the Masked Humper.

You had to be in the mind of the security guard during those months, as somebody kept making their way into the ring, humping members of the promotion. The Masked Humper, as we called them, seemed relentless in their pranks, and it was starting to make the security guard look bad. You could tell he had reached his breaking point, and he was determined to catch the culprit.

It's one of my most favorite times of a prank gone wrong. To this day, me and the others involved still laugh about it. The best part is that it was a harmless yet fun prank that only a handful of us knew about. In pro wrestling, these kinds of shenanigans are what hold people together. They create bonds, memories, and stories that we can look back on and laugh at years later.

In the world of pro wrestling, ribs and pranks have become a time-honored tradition that brings laughter among the wrestlers. From my experiences on the road and in various promotions, I've come to appreciate the art of pulling off a well-executed rib. It's not about causing harm or discomfort, but rather about creating fun, memorable moments that everyone can share and laugh about. Ribs are a way for wrestlers to bond, build friendships, and develop a strong sense of comradery within the locker room. These light-hearted pranks often serve as a rite of passage, signifying acceptance and belonging among the boys. While they may seem mischievous on the surface, ribs foster an atmosphere of trust and mutual respect among those who partake in these playful antics.

In the high-pressure world of pro wrestling, where physicality and competition can be intense, ribs provide a much-needed release and bring a sense of joy to the business. They remind us not to take ourselves too seriously and to cherish the moments of laughter and friendship shared behind the scenes.

Chapter 12
Wrestling Ring Legends:
Battling Ho's and Kings!

Wrestling against big names from the past has been a dream come true for me. To step into the ring with wrestlers I grew up watching on TV is an indescribable feeling. It's a testament to the opportunities that indy wrestling can offer and the impact that the wrestling community has on the careers of up-and-coming talent.

Not only did I have the chance to face legendary wrestlers from major promotions, but I also got to learn from them in the process. Being in the same locker room with these veterans and hearing their stories has been incredibly inspiring and educational. It has taught me valuable lessons about the history of the business and the dedication it takes to succeed in this industry. Every time I wrestled against a big name, it pushed me to elevate my game. It challenged me to bring my best and prove myself in the ring. These experiences have not only boosted my confidence but also made me realize that I can hold my own against some of the industry's best.

I'm going to talk about some of my favorite big names I've ever wrestled. Don't think that this is just some local wrestler trying to name-drop; a lot of these matches hold sentimental value in my memories of wrestling. When you get to wrestle a big name, it not only shows that the renowned wrestler you're working against is trusting you with their body, but it also demonstrates that the promotion booking you for the match knows you're more than capable of delivering in a match against someone of such notoriety. It's a big honor.

One of the first major names I ever wrestled was Marty Jannetty. If you aren't aware, he was formerly Shawn Michaels' tag team partner as part of the Rockers. They were former WWE tag team champions, and he became famous for being betrayed by Shawn

Michaels and thrown through the barbershop window in an infamous moment. I had the incredible opportunity to wrestle him in 2009 when he was in the middle of a career rebirth. Around that time, he was actually wrestling on WWE TV, reuniting with HBK on TV, wrestling Kurt Angle on a Smackdown episode, and even facing The Miz. He was on fire at the time, and I have to tell you, he was one cool cat, to use a cliche.

Wrestling Jannetty was amazing!

When I walked into the locker room and went to introduce myself, it felt like I had known Marty Jannetty for years. He was very friendly and even asked who was going over, which was hilarious considering he's a former WWE Intercontinental Champion. I replied, "Sir, of course you're going over." Then I asked him what he wanted to do in the match, and he surprised me by saying, "You can do whatever you want."

It was a rare opportunity because usually, legends and old-timers like to call the whole match themselves. However, Marty let me put the match together, and I have to tell you, we did a lot of stuff - more than I would have expected. We incorporated sunset flips, cross bodys, suplexes, spots with our valets and managers on the outside, super kicks, and so much more. The match turned out to be an action-packed 20-plus-minute encounter, and it was an incredible experience.

The situation with Marty Jannetty was both surprising and inspiring. Before we stepped into the ring, he confided in me about his injured ankles, which urgently needed surgery. He made a heartfelt request, asking me not to disclose this information to anyone since it could jeopardize his chances of working with WWE. It was evident that he was willing to push through the pain to deliver a great match for the fans.

As we prepared for our bout, Marty's professionalism and dedication shone through. Despite the discomfort, he was determined to give the audience an unforgettable performance. He encouraged me to take the lead in putting the match together, showing a level of trust and respect that truly honored me as a fellow wrestler.

When it was time to hit the ring, Marty took it upon himself to lift his spirits in a unique way. Chugging two beers and taking some Tylenol, he masked the pain and displayed his warrior spirit, ready to give his all for the fans. As I said, our match turned out to be an action-packed affair, filled with Sunset flips, cross bodys, suplexes and even super kicks.

Experiencing Marty Jannetty's entrance was a surreal moment for me. As soon as his iconic WWE theme song, the classic Rockers' tune, hit the arena, a rush of excitement and nostalgia washed over me. It was like witnessing a living legend in action, and I couldn't help but get goosebumps all over my arms. My tag partner at the time, Dalton, shared the same sentiment, and we both knew we were about to create an unforgettable memory.

Marty's energy and enthusiasm were contagious as he made his way to the ring, performing his trademark Rockers run and high-fiving everyone along the way. Seeing him up close, it was hard to believe the years that had passed since his prime. As the bell rang, the match began, and Marty's commitment to his craft was evident from the get-go.

Despite the condition of his injured ankles, Marty displayed an incredible level of resilience and determination. He moved with a grace and skill that belied his age, showcasing why he had been a true standout in the wrestling world. He pushed himself to go beyond what most would have expected, putting on a fast-paced and high-impact performance that left a lasting impression on me and the audience.

Marty was an absolute professional!

After the show, Marty Jannetty surprised us all by lending a hand in putting the ring back together. It's not often you see someone with his level of fame and experience getting involved in the setup process, but Marty was different. Despite being a seasoned wrestler with WrestleMania appearances and international recognition, he remained down-to-earth and approachable.

His willingness to help with the ring setup showed a remarkable level of humility and respect for the wrestling business. It was a true testament to his character and professionalism, and it left a lasting impression on everyone present that night. Seeing a wrestling legend like Marty Jannetty actively participating in the setup alongside local talents reminded us that no matter how successful one becomes, staying grounded and being a team player is crucial.

Wrestling Viscera, also known as King Mabel, was a surreal experience for me, especially considering his long and storied career with WWE. On October 4th, 2008, he had recently departed from WWE and was venturing through the independent circuit with NWA. Our showdown unfolded in Robstown, Texas. It was a handicap match, with my tag partner Andy Dalton by my side.

Viscera's size and presence in the ring were awe-inspiring, but what struck me the most was his kind and friendly demeanor outside the squared circle. Despite his intimidating wrestling persona, he turned out to be the sweetest big man I had ever encountered in the industry. He carried himself with genuine humility, and it was an honor to share the ring with him. Tragically, Viscera has since passed away, leaving behind a lasting legacy in the world of professional wrestling.

Wrestling Viscera was truly an unforgettable experience, and his presence in the ring was larger than life. When he made his way to the ring, he commanded everyone's attention, towering over everyone with his imposing stature. But what struck me the most was how surprisingly gentle and friendly he was in the ring, despite his intimidating persona. I found Viscera to be one of the safest and most considerate opponents I've ever wrestled, especially considering his immense size and strength. His chops and moves were delivered with such precision that I barely felt a thing, and even when he executed a powerful backdrop on me, it felt like landing on a cloud.

During our match, I had the opportunity to witness his skill and professionalism firsthand. His black hole slam dropping my tag team partner, Dalton, on me barely affected me, and that's a testament to his ability to protect his opponents while still putting on an impressive show. Wrestling Viscera was a humbling experience, and it shattered any preconceived notions I may have had about working with big guys in the industry.

Viscera's unique combination of being the safest and softest big man in the ring and his larger-than-life love gimmick truly made him one of a kind. Spending time with him after the show was just as enjoyable as wrestling him in the ring. His charisma and charm seemed to extend beyond the wrestling world, and it's no surprise that the ladies at the gentleman's club loved him.

Wrestling Viscera in the NWA was a big moment!

As for his love for Whataburger, that's definitely a legendary and fun fact! It's clear that Viscera had a great sense of humor and knew how to enjoy life to the fullest. Stopping at every Whataburger on the way to Robstown Texas must have been quite the adventure for the guys, and it's little moments like these that create lasting memories in the wrestling business.

Viscera's personality and presence left a lasting impact not only on those he wrestled with but also on the people he interacted with outside the ring. It's heartwarming to hear stories of him being so well-liked and remembered fondly by those who had the pleasure of knowing him. He may have left us too soon, but his legacy as a beloved wrestler and a kind-hearted individual lives on in the hearts of those he touched.

Throughout my wrestling career, I've had the incredible opportunity to face many talented opponents, making it difficult to choose just a few that stand out in my mind. Among them are my encounters with my friends Shawn Hernandez and his tag team partner Homicide, famously known as LAX in Impact Wrestling. We shared the ring on multiple occasions, and those matches were undeniably enjoyable and filled with lasting memories. Wrestling alongside people you genuinely get along with adds an extra layer of excitement to the sport, even though it remains a competitive business.

Homicide from LAX giving me the Cop Killa

Shawn Hernandez and Homicide, as LAX, are undoubtedly one of the best tag teams in pro wrestling history, and facing them was an honor. Their skills, chemistry, and the popularity they had at that time created an electrifying atmosphere inside the ring. It was a thrilling challenge to go up against such seasoned professionals, and each encounter provided a valuable learning experience for me in the business. The mutual respect between us contributed to the overall enjoyment and the growth of each match.

Wrestling James Ellsworth and WWE Hall of Famer Rikishi were truly memorable experiences in my career. James Ellsworth gained fame for his unique look and his surprising victories over AJ Styles, which became iconic moments in WWE history. Facing off against him on May 4th, 2018, proved to be a delightful and engaging bout, with his comedic persona adding an extra touch of originality to the match. His involvement with women's wrestling also made him a significant figure in the industry.

Rikishi, on the other hand, is a legendary figure in professional wrestling, known for his larger-than-life persona and his signature move, the Stink face. Being part of a tag match on March 10th, 2017, alongside a distinguished Hall of Famer, was a truly honorable experience. And yes, I can proudly say that I took the infamous Stink face, which has become an iconic moment in Rikishi's career. Wrestling someone of Rikishi's caliber is an extraordinary experience, and I learned a lot from being in the ring with him.

The opportunity to wrestle against the legendary "Hacksaw" Jim Duggan was truly extraordinary. I had the privilege of facing off against this icon in a singles match on November 4th, 2016. He truly embodies his character both on and off-screen. Meeting him backstage, he exudes a lovable and approachable personality, making everyone around him laugh and smile. And when you step into the ring with him, it becomes an absolute spectacle. His iconic "HOOOOO!" battle cry and his trusty 2x4 add to the electrifying atmosphere, captivating the audience and creating an unforgettable moment in the squared circle.

What makes Hacksaw stand out is not just his gimmick but his genuine persona that shines through both in and out of the ring. Fans can't help but be drawn to his infectious energy and larger-than-life personality. In the ring, Hacksaw brings a unique mix of power and agility, making his matches entertaining and engaging to watch. His matches are often filled with electrifying moments, and he knows how to connect with the crowd, making them feel like they are a part of the action. His natural charisma and ability to interact with the audience turn each match into a memorable experience.

As I was climbing up the ranks in wrestling, I closely studied matches of legendary figures like Hacksaw Jim Duggan. It struck me that many of these wrestling icons, such as Ric Flair, Bret Hart, Sting, and Hulk Hogan, had their signature sequences of moves that they would incorporate into their matches consistently. It's like they had a well-choreographed dance with the audience, where each move played a crucial role in creating an emotional connection with the fans. Seeing these greats execute their familiar spots with precision and flair not only entertained the crowd but also allowed the audience to actively participate in the excitement by cheering along and recognizing the iconic maneuvers they witnessed on television.

Wrestling Hacksaw was surreal!

"Hacksaw" Jim Duggan was undoubtedly a master of his craft, and stepping into the ring with him was an awe-inspiring experience. Having admired him throughout my wrestling journey, getting the chance to wrestle him was a dream come true. In person, he exuded the same lovable and charismatic persona that he portrayed on TV. It was an absolute thrill to share the squared circle with someone I looked up to and respected. Wrestling against Hacksaw taught me valuable lessons about ring psychology and how to engage and entertain the audience. Every move he made seemed to carry a sense of purpose, and his ability to connect with the crowd was truly remarkable.

Moreover, what made the experience even more special was the genuine appreciation and encouragement I received from Hacksaw himself. As a young wrestler, receiving compliments and positive feedback from a veteran like him meant the world to me. His words of praise were a tremendous confidence booster and reaffirmed my passion for the sport.

Jerry "The King" Lawler was unquestionably a dream opponent for me. Stepping into the ring with him on November 2nd, 2018, fulfilled an experience I had always cherished. When it comes to notable journeyman wrestlers, aside from the Nature Boy Ric Flair,

Lawler stands out as a true legend and a master of his craft. His work in the wrestling industry has been nothing short of exceptional, and I looked up to him as a role model for his in-ring prowess and captivating storytelling abilities.

Leading up to the match, I had the added excitement of teaming up with a partner who portrayed a king gimmick. We used this to our advantage, leveraging the king personas to draw heat from the crowd and set the stage for an intense encounter. As the moment to step into the ring with Lawler approached, a mix of nerves and exhilaration filled me. However, I received a piece of advice that added an extra layer of responsibility to the match. Lawler's wife, who was also his business manager at the time, warned me to be cautious while moving him around in the ring to avoid any potential injuries. The thought of accidentally hurting such a revered wrestling legend immediately put fear in me, but it also heightened my determination to execute the match flawlessly.

When the match finally began, it was time, and all my focus shifted to delivering a performance worthy of sharing the ring with "The King." Despite the initial nerves, we soon found ourselves in a rhythm, walking and talking in the ring, creating a captivating story for the audience. The chemistry between us was electric, and I made sure to handle Lawler with the utmost care, respecting his legendary status while still engaging in a competitive and entertaining contest. The match ended with Jerry hitting me with a Stone Cold Stunner that garnered a huge pop, as Colt Cabana came in and accidentally hit me with a chain.

It was an honor to be able to wrestle Jerry Lawler!

The way I got Jerry Lawler booked to wrestle me in that match was actually quite unexpected. I happened to run into him when I was driving through Memphis with my friend Jay, and I decided to stop at one of his barbecue restaurants. To my surprise, he was sitting right there at a table, casually signing autographs for people. I couldn't pass up the opportunity, so I approached him, expressed my admiration for his work, and mentioned that I was a professional wrestler. During our conversation, he inquired if I had any connections or contacts in Texas wrestling. Without hesitation, I told him that I did, and I took down his contact information. In due time, everything fell into alignment, and he was scheduled to face me for the match on November 2nd, 2018, in San Antonio, Texas. As I mentioned earlier, this was an exceptionally memorable experience.

Jerry "The King" Lawler is an absolute legend in the world of professional wrestling. When you delve into his incredible history, it's truly awe-inspiring to think that I'm one of the potentially thousands of opponents he's faced throughout his storied career. It's an unimaginable honor, and I feel incredibly blessed to have been given the opportunity to step into the ring with such a seasoned and iconic performer.

Wrestling against Jerry Lawler was a dream come true, and it's an experience that will forever hold a special place in my heart. His knowledge, skill, and charisma are unmatched, and being part of his long list of opponents is a testament to my dedication and passion for the sport. Sharing the ring with him taught me invaluable lessons and elevated my own wrestling abilities to new heights.

Being in the presence of a true legend like Lawler is humbling, and it motivates me to continue pushing myself to improve and make a mark in the wrestling world. It's moments like these that remind me why I love this business and reinforce the importance of respecting and learning from those who have paved the way before me. Wrestling against "The King" is an experience I will cherish forever, and it inspires me to keep pursuing my dreams in this incredible sport.

Wrestling against name talent is always a highlight for me, as it reflects the promotion's belief in my abilities to step up against well-known wrestlers. It's a confidence boost knowing that they trust me to deliver an exciting and competitive match against established names. One of the most thrilling aspects of the indy wrestling scene is the element of surprise. You never know who might be the next breakout star, and it's incredible to see wrestlers from Texas secure contracts with renowned companies like Impact Wrestling and AEW. Over the years, I've had the opportunity to wrestle both male and female talents who later went on to achieve great success, adding to the excitement of being part of the Indies.

I always get asked who my dream opponents that I haven't wrestled yet are. Having a dream match against the Nature Boy Ric Flair is something that I've always wished for deep in my heart. He's an icon in the wrestling world, and even though it seems unlikely due to his retirement, I can't help but imagine how incredible that experience would be. Ric Flair's mastery of psychology and old-school planning in his matches has been an inspiration for me throughout my career.

My dream match would be against Ric Flair.

If by some miracle, I ever got the chance to step into the ring with Ric Flair, I know I would be in awe and marking out like a true fan. His presence, charisma and unmatched in-ring abilities have left an indelible mark on the industry, making him one of the greatest wrestlers of all time. I can only imagine the level of intensity and excitement that would fill the arena during that dream match. When I step up to the mic, I can't help but channel my inner Ric Flair. He's an absolute legend and an icon, the greatest of all time in my book. If I had the chance, wrestling against Macho Man and Sting would have been a dream come true. Nevertheless, I feel incredibly blessed to have wrestled some incredible talents like Janetty, Hacksaw, Jerry Lawler and many others. Each match has been a humbling experience, and I genuinely feel honored to have shared the ring with these greats.

I know it may sound like I'm name-dropping. Wrestling these legends has taught me so much and has motivated me to keep pushing myself in this business. There's still a long list of talented wrestlers out there, especially in the Indies, whom I haven't had the chance to work with yet. It's exciting to think about the potential opportunities that lie ahead. One day, I hope to step into the ring with even more incredible talents, learning from them and creating unforgettable moments together.

Chapter 13
Favorite Matches & Crazy Moments: From Light Tubes to Easter Eggs

I've had the chance to be a part of quite a few wrestling matches that have stuck with me over time. Now, just to clarify, when I say "memorable," I don't necessarily mean they were all amazing. The real essence of the Indy scene is all about those moments that you can hardly believe are real. You know, the times when you're there and you're witnessing stuff that's just... unbelievable.

This can cover a wide range of things. We're talking about rings that weren't put together all that well, wrestlers who were still learning the ropes, and venues that might not have seemed entirely legit. And let's not forget the interesting mix of people who show up to watch these shows.

What makes the Indy scene so intriguing isn't just the top-notch wrestling, but the unfiltered and sometimes downright surprising experiences. It's a world where you're faced with the unexpected, where things aren't always as they seem, and where you find yourself in situations that feel like they're straight out of a dream.

The world of pro wrestling is like a big, lively circus, full of ups and downs. I've seen my share of both good and bad in this business, and honestly, I don't even know where to start. But I want to share some of the most interesting stories I've collected along the way.

In the world of pro wrestling, there's a mix of experiences. Some moments stand out as fantastic, showing the incredible side of the wrestling scene. Others serve as reminders that this industry has its challenges. So, let me dive into sharing a few captivating stories that have stuck with me. These tales offer a glimpse into the unpredictable and captivating world of pro wrestling that I've been a part of.

Wrestling isn't always about glitz and glam; there's a particular memory that stands out vividly. Partnered with another wrestler named Jacob Ladder, we made a deliberate choice to journey down to Rio Bravo on June 29th, 2004. This quaint town rests in the Texas valley, right along the border with Mexico. To be honest, I hadn't even heard of this place before. Now, the promotion that invited us to wrestle there did sound a bit sketchy, but the offer on the table was tempting – they were offering us good money to come and put in the work. So, without much ado, we both decided, "Why not? Let's go for the payday."

As we made our way to the destination, the journey itself became a bit of an adventure. We're driving along, and the landscape starts getting more and more rural. We're out in the sticks, miles away from what we're used to. All the while, Jacob and I are exchanging glances like, "Where on earth are we headed?"

And then, the moment of revelation arrives. We're driving, and suddenly, out of nowhere, we spot this sight to our right that's etched into my memory. I kid you not, it's this dilapidated, shoddy-looking chicken coop shack, standing in all its glory. But that's not even the best part – right next to this ramshackle structure is a wrestling ring. Yes, you heard me right, a wrestling ring. But here's the kicker: the ropes of this ring are nothing more than garden hoses. I couldn't believe my eyes.

So, picture this – we've traveled all this way to a town we've never heard of, come across what seems like the world's most poorly constructed chicken coop, and right next to it is this makeshift wrestling ring with garden hoses for ropes. It was a surreal moment, a true testament to the bizarre and unexpected experiences that you encounter in the world of indy wrestling.

After we managed to park the car, we stepped out and had a bit of a pep talk. We reminded ourselves that despite the questionable setting, this gig promised a decent payday. With a mix of "why the fuck are we doing this?" and apprehension, we made our way towards the heart of the event. As we approached, the promoter greeted us with a self-satisfied grin that you couldn't miss from a mile away. It was as if he was beaming with pride over the spectacle he'd put together.

With that characteristic grin still plastered on his face, the promoter led us towards the wrestling ring. This was the centerpiece of his creation, and he couldn't have been prouder. As we stood there, taking in the sight, he motioned for us to come closer, inviting us into his world. "Welcome to my show," he proclaimed, almost bursting with enthusiasm.

But the true adventure was yet to unfold. With an air of intrigue, he motioned for us to follow him further. He took us inside what could only be described as a damaged shed, which was the same structure that had caught our attention earlier. This shed, as we were about to discover, was the infamous chicken coop he had mentioned earlier.

With a sense of anticipation, he gestured towards a rather curious sight. There, laid out on the ground, was a box spring mattress that seemed out of place in this already bizarre scene. What caught our eyes, however, were the water hose ropes haphazardly wrapped around the mattress. It was an odd sight to behold, and the promoter seemed keen to fill us in on the backstory. "Last show, we had a three-way dance right here in this little ring," he explained, his excitement though the roof.

As the words sunk in, I couldn't help but marvel at the sheer audacity of it all. The absurdity of the situation, the disgusting setting, and the promoter's unbridled enthusiasm – it was all so uniquely indy wrestling.

I turned to Ladder and just said, "Dude, I'm never coming back here after this." It was like a mix of disbelief and humor on my face. But you know what? The night turned out to be pretty wild, despite all the doubts we had.

So there we were, Ladder and I, in the world of Rio Bravo wrestling that night. And, I've got to admit, our match wasn't half bad. The ring was a bit sketchy, and those ropes were made from water hoses? Yeah, not exactly your usual setup. They had this weird flexibility that we weren't used to, so we had to get creative with our moves.

But you know what the cool part was? Despite the odd circumstances, Ladder and I put on a really good show. It's like we turned the challenges of that makeshift ring into opportunities. And you want to know why we gelled so well? We had a bunch of matches together at Rudy Boys before, so we knew each other's rhythm inside out.

Honestly, we made that ring work for us. It's like we had this unspoken understanding, and every move just flowed. And when the match wrapped up and the dust settled, Ladder and I exchanged this look like, "Yeah, we did it." We took this iffy situation and turned it into a win. I know earlier I was saying I'd never come back, but looking back, that night in Rio Bravo, weird as it was, ended up being one of those moments that stick with you.

During my wrestling career, I was fortunate enough to square off against a few Japanese wrestlers, one of whom was Kazushi Miyamoto. He had a stint in Total Nonstop Action Wrestling (TNA) and had also graced the ring of All Japan Pro Wrestling. Back then, he was embracing a fantastic Muta-esque persona known as the Great Kazushi. What really stands out, aside from his in-ring prowess, was his personality off-stage.

When you encountered Kazushi behind the scenes, you'd find a genuinely affable individual. He had this quiet demeanor about him that carried an air of intimidation at times. However, it didn't take long to realize that beneath that exterior was a person who was quite easygoing and even-keeled.

Working with Kazushi was something I cherished, especially considering the mutual rapport we shared. If he took a liking to you, which I was fortunate enough to experience, collaborating with him was an absolute pleasure. His professionalism and willingness to create compelling matches were truly admirable.

However, if you happened to find yourself on the other side of his preference, well, that's when his demeanor could signal something different. Kazushi wasn't one to mince words; his expression and attitude would often speak volumes. Yet, even in those instances, there was something straightforward and honest about him – you always knew where you stood.

Following our initial match on May 18th, 2005, I felt a deep sense of honor when I discovered that Kazushi Miyamoto had genuinely enjoyed it. Even more remarkable was his consistent desire to face me in subsequent matches, which carried significant weight for me. There were times when his scheduled opponents would cancel at the last minute, and I'd step in at his request. It was a unique partnership that started forming.

I have to admit, Kazushi pushed me in ways I didn't expect. He'd make me work really hard and even do moves that were outside my comfort zone, like moon salts and other high-flying stuff. It was challenging, but it made me grow as a wrestler. It was through this experience that I began to gain the trust of other promoters when it came to wrestling wrestlers who didn't speak English.

These moments were about more than just wrestling. They shaped my career in unexpected ways. Wrestling with Kazushi taught me to step out of my boundaries and try new things in the ring. The skills I gained from those matches expanded my horizons and made me a more versatile performer.

And you know, it wasn't just about impressing Kazushi; it was about the connections we built and the doors that opened as a result. The trust he had in my ability to communicate through wrestling led to more opportunities with international talents. It's really a reminder of how wrestling can bridge gaps and bring people together, no matter where they're from.

Let me share a humorous anecdote from that period. On September 10th, 2005, I had a match with Milano Collection AT, who was temporarily in Texas for training under Rudy's guidance. He would go on to become a prominent figure in Japanese wrestling, but during that time, he was honing his skills in the American style.

So, during our match, things were going smoothly. At a certain point, I signaled to Milano for him to take over the match. I was ready for us to do the planned cutoff spot that we had worked out. But here's the twist – Milano had a different idea in mind.

Without any hesitation, he unexpectedly launched a quick and precise kick right to my groin. It was like a shoot-style move, something that wasn't part of the plan. I was caught totally off guard. The pain was intense, and I was momentarily stunned by the shock of it. I doubled over, trying to recover from the surprise blow. The sensation was so intense that I felt dizzy for a moment. I was really close to passing out from the sudden pain.

What adds a humorous twist to this tale is that the incident took place during an event where Al Snow was conducting a wrestling clinic and seminar. Later that evening, he was scheduled to provide feedback on all our matches. So, with that context in mind, when our match wrapped up and we returned backstage, Mr. Snow himself made his presence felt.

He didn't waste any time expressing his thoughts, and with a mix of amusement and disbelief, he commented on the unexpected kick to the groin.

"Geez, that kick to the nuts was brutal," he quipped. He even went on to joke that if he were in my shoes, he might have promptly called an end to the match right then and there.

It was a lighthearted remark, but it perfectly encapsulated the shock value of that particular moment. Al Snow's candid reaction to the unconventional move mirrored the sentiments that I, and probably everyone else present, had experienced in that split second.

Earlier in this book, I briefly mentioned Xtreme Championship Wrestling (XCW), a wrestling promotion where I had the opportunity to wrestle from 2007 to 2008. This promotion was based in Denton, Texas. At that time, XCW held a TV slot on a channel called MAV TV, and their DVDs were even being sold at Best Buy stores. One of the notable events they organized annually was called "Battle Box," which had a Hardcore theme to it.

In my initial encounter with Battle Box on April 4th, 2008, I found myself tasked with participating in a light tube ladder match. This is a match where the ring is surrounded by actual light tubes. Admittedly, there was a mix of excitement and trepidation in the air as I contemplated what lay ahead. The thought of being involved in a match where light tubes were involved as weapons was indeed a bit intimidating.

The XCW Light tube Match was insane!

However, something within me shifted as I considered the broader context. The realization that this event was being broadcast on TV and pay-per-view and that their DVDs were being sold at Best Buy stores struck me. It was a moment that made me rethink my approach. I recognized that this was an opportunity to leave a lasting impact, to contribute something truly memorable to an event that had a broader reach than just the live audience.

With that in mind, my perspective changed. The nervousness was still there, but it was accompanied by a newfound determination. I saw this match as a chance to showcase something exceptional, something that would stand out in the minds of viewers who might stumble upon it on television or at the store. It was about more than just my personal performance; it was about contributing to the legacy of XCW's Battle Box event.

In this particular match, not only myself but all of my opponents were in agreement from the get-go – we were going to take things to the extreme. Our goal was to create a truly wild and intense spectacle, one that involved a fair amount of bloodshed. To achieve this, we hatched a plan: at intervals of around 20 minutes, we'd take a shot and consume aspirin. The idea behind this strategy was to make our bodies more susceptible to bleeding, setting the stage for a dramatic and chaotic encounter.

Once we stepped into the ring, all prior agreements went out the window. It was like a no-holds-barred scenario, where the only limits were the ones we chose to impose on ourselves. I distinctly remember that I had never bled so profusely in my life. Now, I've never been particularly fond of hardcore wrestling

– while I can definitely appreciate it when executed skillfully, this particular match stands out as a questionable decision in hindsight.

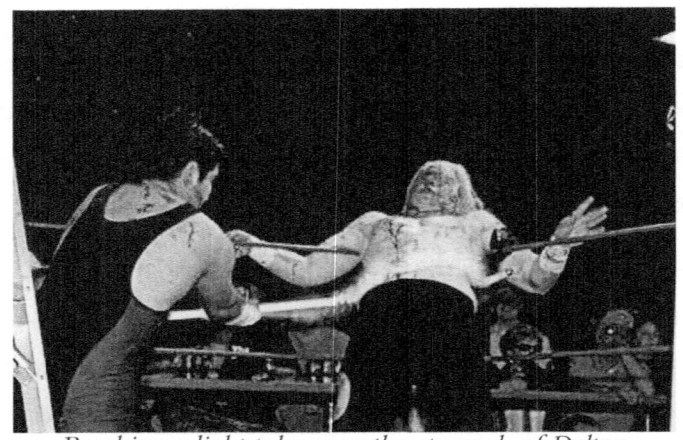

Breaking a light tube over the stomach of Dalton

Despite my reservations, I have to concede that when you see the video footage, there's an undeniable sense of awe that comes with witnessing the chaotic spectacle we created. However, that doesn't change the fact that, personally, it ranks as one of the riskier endeavors I've undertaken. In our fervor to deliver something visually striking, we threw caution to the wind, neglecting our own safety in the process.

Indeed, I found myself carved up and nursing a fair amount of pain afterward. The impact of the light tubes themselves hitting you isn't as intense as one might think. It's when those tubes shatter and the shards of glass scatter around that things take a treacherous turn. The aftermath was far from glamorous, as the broken glass posed a genuine hazard. The aesthetic value of the visual spectacle came with a hefty price tag in terms of discomfort and potential injuries.

Following the match, my bleeding was relentless, and it reached a point where I had no choice but to seek a remedy. The solution, somewhat unconventional, involved heading over to the promoter's house for a swift shower. However, the challenge was apparent the moment I stepped out of the shower – the bleeding was far from abated. It seemed that no matter what I did, my own blood kept finding its way back onto me.

This resulted in an unexpectedly prolonged stay in the shower, as I attempted to curtail the continuous stream of blood that marked my body. In retrospect, I realize that opting for this makeshift solution might not have been the wisest choice. Looking back, a visit to the hospital probably would have been the more prudent path to take. Stitching up the wound on my back seemed a reasonable course of action, but I chose instead to simply patch it up as best I could and leave it at that.

During that time, something both sad and strangely funny happened involving my girlfriend Kristen. It was a mix of emotions and unexpected events that left us both a bit puzzled and amused. So, after the match was over, I was pretty oblivious to what was happening in the crowd. Little did I know, Kristen was there, in tears and visibly upset. The match had affected her deeply because of its intense brutality.

Once the match wrapped up, Kristen mustered the courage to come and check on me. And this is where things got interesting. Brian, a security guard who happened to be a friend of mine, decided to play a prank on her. He casually told Kristen that I had been taken to the emergency room as a joke. He probably thought it was harmless fun, but little did he know how it would snowball. So there was Kristen, in a state of panic, trying to figure out where I was and how to get to me to make sure I was okay. She was completely worried and just trying to find any information she could.

When I finally made it back from the promoter's house, I went up to Kristen to say hi. But instead of a warm greeting, I was met with a mix of relief and frustration. She was pretty upset, asking me why I would lie about being at the ER. I was totally taken aback since I had no clue what was going on. It turns out that Brian's little prank had caused quite a bit of chaos in Kristen's mind. Even though she didn't contact hospitals, she was definitely in a panicked state, trying to figure out where I was and if I was okay.

This particular match remains etched in my memory as a truly unforgettable experience. It stands as a testament to my toughness and determination, serving as evidence that I was indeed as tough as they come. More than that, it felt like a crucial moment that signaled my readiness to progress to the next level within XCW.

It's worth noting that this wrestling promotion had a distinct hardcore focus, making it a fitting platform for a match of this intensity. The fact that the event was rooted in a hardcore wrestling ethos lent even more significance to my performance that day. The impact wasn't just on the audience, but it had a ripple effect among my peers as well.

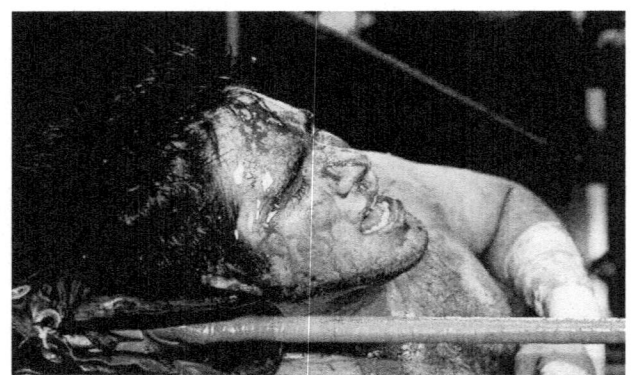

I was a bloody mess after the light tube match.

Even Masada, a notable figure in the hardcore wrestling scene, recognized the effort I had put forth. He took the time to acknowledge my performance and offer his commendation. His approval was a moment of validation that resonated deeply.

Regrettably, this event didn't get the opportunity to reach a broader audience through its inclusion in DVDs available at Best Buy. This unfortunate turn of events was due to the expiration of the distribution deal with Best Buy, a detail unbeknownst to us at the time. Nevertheless, the absence of the match from that particular platform didn't diminish its significance. It remained a standout match for me, an embodiment of the hardcore wrestling spirit that defined the promotion.

After we got cleaned up, we crashed at Danny and Scott's for the evening and I remember lying there with Kristen. I couldn't sleep because my back was sliced up, but I remember holding her while she slept. Kristen truly exemplified what it meant to be a good sport. Many times, the guys would playfully tease and deliberately provoke her, and I must admit that I even found myself engaging in this banter on occasion. Despite all of this, she consistently displayed a remarkable level of patience and good humor. It was a quality that set her apart and earned her my utmost respect.

One of the ways Kristen showed her unwavering support was by frequently hitting the road with me. She willingly embarked on those long journeys, accompanying me to wrestling events. This wasn't just about sharing the physical space; it was a testament to her commitment and dedication to being a part of my world. Her presence provided comfort, companionship, and a connection that helped alleviate the demands and pressures that came with the wrestling lifestyle.

Moreover, Kristen wasn't merely a companion on the road; she extended her support beyond that. When the rigors of wrestling left me physically drained or in need of assistance, she was right there to lend a helping hand. Her caring nature and willingness to take care of me during those moments of fatigue or injury made her an indispensable part of my journey. Beyond the tangible support, Kristen was undeniably my biggest fan. Her enthusiasm and encouragement were a constant source of motivation. Whether in the stands cheering loudly or in the quiet moments of reflection, her belief in me served as a powerful driving force.

In retrospect, I am genuinely grateful for everything Kristen contributed to my wrestling career and personal life. Her ability to navigate the world of wrestling, her resilience in the face of playful taunts, her companionship on the road, and her unwavering support both physically and emotionally – all of these facets combined to form a solid foundation of encouragement and comfort. She was more than just a companion; she was an essential support system that uplifted me during both triumphant and challenging times.

The relationship we shared wasn't just about her being in my corner – it was a true partnership that underscored the value of understanding, respect, and mutual support. As I reflect on those times, I'm reminded of how vital it is to have individuals like Kristen in one's life, individuals who go above and beyond to champion your dreams and well-being.

Reflecting on that period, it's quite apparent that I was far from my best self, especially when it came to handling matters within the wrestling business. In all honesty, my level of maturity left much to be desired. In particular, my attitude towards relationships took a wrong turn, a transformation triggered in part by the painful episode involving Nicole years earlier.

It's with a sense of regret that I admit that my behavior, especially towards Kristen, wasn't something I'm proud of. I had let my emotions and past experiences color my approach, causing me to become someone I barely recognized. It wasn't just an attitude shift; it manifested in my actions as well. I wasn't considerate of Kristen's feelings, making decisions that disregarded her emotions – even going so far as to lie to her at times. I was unfaithful to her, and that's something that deeply troubles me when I think about it now.

Despite this turmoil, Kristen remained an embodiment of patience and kindness. She displayed unwavering sweetness even when I probably didn't deserve it. Her steadfast presence in my life meant more than words could convey – she was a constant source of support, even during my moments of recklessness. She was, and still is, my rock.

Between 2007 and 2008, I had the privilege of wrestling in Louisiana with Bayou Independent Wrestling. Amid the array of matches I participated in, there's one tag team match that remains exceptionally clear in my memory—it occurred on August 8th, 2008. This distinctive encounter beautifully showcased the intertwining of professional wrestling's past and present.

In this particular match, I teamed up with my partner Dalton to face off against Danny Matthews and Scott McKenzie. The bout was more than just a competition; it was a collision of legacies and eras. The intriguing aspect that added layers to this contest was the presence of two legendary figures who stood at the helm of our respective teams.

On our side, we were fortunate to have the iconic Skandor Akbar as our manager. Akbar was a true legend in the wrestling world, known for his prowess as both a manager and a wrestler. Opposing us was the equally legendary Danny Hodge, a name that resonates across generations of wrestling enthusiasts. Hodge's storied career was marked by his remarkable accomplishments and unmatched grappling skills.

Being managed by Akbar was an honor!

What made this match even more captivating was the historical context that surrounded our managers. Skandor Akbar and Danny Hodge had crossed paths and rivalries that stretched back decades, harking back to the old-school territory days. Their narratives were etched in wrestling history, and the clash between them was a reminiscence of the bygone era.

The story line of our match was built on the foundation of their long-standing feud. This encounter was conceived as a final showdown, a last opportunity for Akbar and Hodge to settle their differences in the ring. However, instead of directly facing off against each other, they chose to channel their rivalry through us – their chosen representatives.

As we stepped into the ring that day, we were aware of the weight of history and legacy that accompanied us. The cheers and jeers from the crowd resonated differently, knowing that the clash before them was more than just a typical tag team match. It was a symbolic passing of the torch from two wrestling icons to a new generation of competitors.

It was truly an amazing experience to be in the presence of both Skandor Akbar and Danny Hodge. Akbar's legendary status in the Texas wrestling scene was no joke – he was a true icon who had left an undeniable mark. And Danny Hodge, well, his reputation as a living legend was something else altogether. I mean, the guy could crush apples with his bare hands – that's the stuff of wrestling folklore.

Getting to share the ring with these two iconic figures was a big deal, to say the least. Akbar's influence went way beyond just wrestling; he was a major player who had made a lasting impact on the whole wrestling world. Hodge, with his unbelievable strength feat, was like a superhero in the wrestling realm.

Out of all the memories from that time, there's one that stands out – a snapshot of me with Danny Hodge. It's a cool reminder of the moment I shared with someone who had accomplished something pretty incredible. It's one of those things you want to keep forever. I do wish I had gotten a picture with Skandor Akbar too, looking back. You know, capturing a moment with a true wrestling legend is something you don't want to miss out on.

The legendary Danny Hodge.

But even without the pictures, the memory of being around them is still vivid and impactful. You could feel the respect and admiration that surrounded both Akbar and Hodge. It was clear they had made a deep impression on the wrestling scene. Standing next to them wasn't just about being physically present; it was like being part of this long line of wrestlers and fans who appreciate the history they've helped create.

When I think back on it, the experience was more than just a cool story. It felt like a connection between different eras of wrestling, like these guys were the bridge between the past and the present. It's a reminder of the legacy they've left behind, and I'm really grateful for the chance to have shared a moment with them.

Another standout tag team match in my wrestling journey was the clash against the formidable pair of Luke Gallows and Mike Knox on June 8th, 2013. These guys weren't just any wrestlers; they were former WWE and Impact Wrestling talents. Luke Gallows, in particular, would later go on to be a part of the iconic Bullet Club alongside AJ Styles and Karl Anderson. But it was in 2013 that I found myself stepping into the ring with these two powerhouses, and what unfolded was quite the spectacle.

Our showdown took the form of a tag team tables match, and the stakes were high. It wasn't just a regular tag team match – we were taking the battle to another level with the addition of tables. What added an interesting twist to the mix was that it was three of us against them, giving us a numerical advantage that we intended to make full use of.

As the match progressed, the action spilled out beyond the confines of the ring. We navigated the entire building, using our surroundings to our advantage. It was a chaotic yet exhilarating experience, as we fought tooth and nail to gain the upper hand against our formidable opponents.

A surprising and entertaining twist came in the form of our referee – a midget who added a unique element to the match. This unexpected choice of referee brought an element of humor and unpredictability, adding a layer of entertainment that only amplified the excitement of the bout.

Luke Gallows tossing tons of chairs on me.

As the match reached its climax, I found myself as the last man standing who hadn't gone through a table yet. But the odds were not in my favor for long. In a dramatic and visually striking moment, both Luke Gallows and Mike Knox teamed up, lifting me high into the air and executing a choke slam that sent me hurtling over the top rope and crashing through not just one, but two tables outside the ring.

The image of that intense moment remains etched in my mind. The collision of bodies, the splintering of tables, and the raw energy of the move created a visual spectacle that was both thrilling and impactful. It was a testament to the adrenaline-fueled chaos of professional wrestling and the lengths we go to create unforgettable moments for the fans.

What truly stood out to me about this particular match was the remarkable attitude displayed by Luke Gallows and Mike Knox. These two towering figures in the world of pro wrestling, with their imposing presence, could have easily taken a different approach. However, what I found most refreshing was their willingness to collaborate, their friendly demeanor, and their humility.

Despite their larger-than-life personas, both Gallows and Knox proved to be remarkably easy to work with. Their approach was devoid of any ego, which is a rarity in a business known for its competitive spirit. They willingly allowed us to execute the maneuvers we wanted against them, a level of cooperation that showcased their dedication to putting on an entertaining match rather than solely seeking to elevate themselves.

It's worth noting that they could have chosen a different path, opting to dominate us in the ring. But their approach was different; they were invested in ensuring that we all had a good time, delivering a match that would be remembered for its excitement and dynamic exchanges. This level of sportsmanship and their genuine enthusiasm for creating a memorable match left a lasting impression on me.

Years down the line, when I had the chance to reminisce about that match with Luke Gallows, we shared a laugh over the unexpected presence of the midget referee. This shared memory served as a testament to the bonds that form among the brotherhood of wrestlers, even in the most unpredictable situations.

During this conversation, Gallows surprised me by offering genuine praise. He acknowledged my role as a heel, highlighting the effort I put into selling for him in the ring. Coming from someone with his experience and stature, this recognition meant a lot to me. It reinforced the idea that even in a business where competition is fierce, mutual respect and a willingness to collaborate can lead to truly remarkable and rewarding experiences.

Participating in a Monster's Ball Match against Abyss from Impact Wrestling on July 6th, 2018, is an experience that truly shines among the highlights of my wrestling journey. To set the stage, a Monster's Ball Match is essentially a no-holds-barred, anything-goes showdown, and this particular one certainly lived up to its reputation. As we stepped into the ring, we knew we were about to create a chaotic spectacle that would push the boundaries of traditional wrestling rules.

This match wasn't your run-of-the-mill bout; it was a canvas for carnage. Thumbtacks, tables, and an array of weapons were at our disposal, turning the ring into an arena of extreme warfare. One particularly fearsome weapon was a board adorned with barbed wire, adding an extra layer of danger to our encounter. The stakes were high, and every hit had the potential to become a game-changer.

Abyss, who was a former Impact Wrestling Champion, brought an aura of dominance to the ring. The fans rallied behind him, solidifying his status as a crowd favorite. At the time, he was also holding the heavyweight championship of the promotion where our match was taking place. This elevated the intensity of our encounter, as the match carried the added significance of being a title bout.

Abyss, a towering presence in Impact Wrestling, personified fear itself. His imposing stature cast a chilling shadow over the ring, striking terror into all, including me—the unfortunate lamb to slaughter that fans anticipated in the looming Monster's Ball match. This was no trifling matter; it was a brutal trial, demanding unwavering resilience as Abyss, with his malevolent aura and sadistic weaponry, redefined brutality.

The energy within the arena was palpable. The crowd's fervor reached an all-time high as they unleashed a torrent of boos directed at me. It was an atmosphere charged with emotion, with the fans firmly aligning themselves against me.

This was super fun because I was playing a "Hollywood" Joey Spector role back then. I lived in Hollywood, California with my friend Carey Martell. I would fly in for the wrestling matches and act all important when I had to promote the matches. You know, California stuff isn't well-liked in Texas, so it stirred up even more excitement. It shows how wrestling can really get people worked up emotionally, making every move and moment feel super important.

Monster's Ball against Abyss was INSANE!

Recalling that match, I can't help but reflect on the sense of exhilaration and fun that accompanied the chaos. The unpredictability of a Monster's Ball Match injects an element of excitement into the proceedings, allowing for moments that push both competitors and the audience to the edge.

As soon as the match kicked off, the intensity was palpable, and we wasted no time in diving head-first into the action. It was a clash of contrasting styles, with his raw power going up against my agility and speed. The dynamic between us set the stage for a thrilling showdown.

Right from the start, he leveraged his strength to gain the upper hand, maneuvering in ways that left me scrambling to keep up. But in a moment that got the crowd cheering, I rebounded off him like a brick wall after attempting a quick cross body. The impact had a certain wow factor, the collision resonating through the arena and eliciting an excited reaction from the spectators.

Despite that exhilarating move, I soon found myself back on the defensive as he reasserted his dominance. Determined to prove my mettle, I resorted to using my wits and strategic thinking to turn the tables.

The back-and-forth nature of the match showcased the tactical chess game that often unfolds inside the wrestling ring.

Realizing that trying to overpower him directly would be an uphill battle, I decided to shift tactics. A well-timed signal to my partners marked a change in our approach. Working as a united front, we launched a coordinated offensive, temporarily overwhelming our opponent. But his sheer strength ultimately proved too much, and he quickly turned the tide. In a stunning display of power, he dispatched one of my partners onto a bed of thumbtacks and sent the other crashing through a table, the impact resonating with a satisfying crash.

The intensity escalated as he unveiled his trademark weapon – Janice, the 2x4 board bristling with menacing nails. It was a symbol of the chaos inherent in a Monster's Ball Match. With a forceful swing, he aimed the weapon at me, and in a heart-pounding moment, I managed to narrowly evade the impending strike, just in the nick of time.

However, the relief was short-lived as he capitalized on the opening, executing a choke slam that drove me right into a board encased in barbed wire.

The sensation of the barbs digging into my skin sent shock waves of pain coursing through me. This unforgettable image highlighted the raw intensity of our confrontation, serving as a reminder that a Monster's Ball Match delivers the kind of raw, unfiltered action that defines wrestling at its most extreme.

During the match, there was a moment that really stood out. I decided to take on the challenge of dealing with the barbed wire without wearing a shirt. Abyss, in his typically candid manner, shared that most wrestlers opt for a shirt under the barbed wire – it sticks to the fabric and adds a layer of protection. But he threw a curve ball at me: he suggested I be the first he wrestles against without a shirt. My response? "Why not? Let's give it a shot." While the barbed wire wasn't the super intense kind that could cause major harm, it was still real enough to deliver some serious pain.

Pressing my bare skin onto that barbed wire wasn't a walk in the park, to put it mildly. The sensation was a sharp reminder that I was deep into a physically demanding match. Even though it wasn't the most hardcore type of barbed wire, the discomfort was no joke, leaving its mark both physically and mentally.

Being choke slammed onto barb wire hurt!

But beyond the barbed wire, the match itself was a thrill. Going up against Abyss, someone I had looked up to and respected, added a special layer of excitement. It's not every day you get the chance to share the ring with someone you've admired from a distance. And what made it even better was the recognition and kind words I got from Abyss after it was all said and done.

What struck me about Abyss was how easy he was to work with. His professionalism and willingness to collaborate made the match flow smoothly. His input and approach played a big role in creating a bout that not only showcased our skills but also gave the fans a memorable show.

When it comes to Texas wrestling, you can't think of a bigger name than the Von Erichs. The Von Erich legacy was practically woven into my early memories. Even as a little kid, my dad and uncles would casually drop Von Erich references whenever wrestling came up in conversation. It's like the Von Erichs were part of the landscape of Texas wrestling, no matter where you turned.

Life has its way of delivering surprises, and on April 12th, 2019, I unexpectedly found myself entering the ring with Hernandez for a tag match against the emerging generation of Von Erichs – Ross and Marshall. Talk about a full-circle moment. The Von Erich name that I'd heard so much about growing up was now a part of my wrestling journey in a very real and personal way.

It's interesting to note that Ross and Marshall had flown in from Hawaii, and the jet lag was definitely making itself known. However, when it was time to shine, you could feel the excitement in the air. We were all ready to put on a show that blended the classic wrestling style with our own modern twists. The match was like a bridge between wrestling's roots and its current evolution, a balance that made it truly special.

Me and Shawn at the mercy of the Von Erich Claw!

Against the odds, Hernandez and I managed to snag the victory. And, funnily enough, I got to score the pin fall. So, of course, I couldn't resist a bit of playful bragging – I mean, I had technically pinned a Von Erich, right?

If you happen to be in Texas, and you're squaring off against someone from the Von Erich lineage in a wrestling match, get ready for a truly magical experience. The crowd's energy, a solid 100% thrown behind the Von Erich family name, speaks volumes about the incredible legacy they've built. I still remember this one time when I stepped into the ring and executed a basic yet effective combo: a tackle, a smooth drop down, a slick hip toss, and then a flawless drop kick. The crowd's reaction? It was as if they thought a gunshot had gone off in the arena. That's how intense and amazing the crowd was that night – a testament to the deep bond between the Von Erichs and their fans.

It's worth mentioning that by this point, my partner Hernandez and I had already racked up quite a bit of experience as a tag team. We had our fair share of tag titles under our belts. So, the chance to go up against well-known opponents while teaming up with my best buddy in the wrestling business was beyond awesome. This whole experience added another layer of meaning to the match – a memorable moment in my wrestling journey that I'll always treasure.

Looking back on that experience, it hits me just how deep wrestling's history runs and how it can intersect with our own lives. That match was like a nod to the timeless Von Erich legacy, a legacy that spans generations and keeps shaping Texas wrestling and beyond.

Chapter 14
Passing the Torch:
Shaping Wrestling's Future

Being a part of the wrestling business now brings me a truly rewarding aspect: the opportunity to train the future stars. I had a taste of this back in 2012 and 2013 when I was connected with a wrestling school for a promotion I was working with at the time. During those years, I had the chance to mentor and train a few students who went on to achieve significant success.

During that period, we even crafted a wrestling angle that had me issuing challenges to every student who had emerged from that Academy. Every single show, I would step into the ring with a different student until this buildup culminated in a gauntlet match —a memorable spectacle where I faced off against each and every one of them in succession. It was an exhilarating experience as these youngsters showcased impressive skills and abilities.

I sincerely hope that whatever knowledge and techniques they acquired from our time together have remained with them and served them well. It's heartening to note that some of these students are still actively engaged in the wrestling world today. Observing their ongoing success over the years has been truly gratifying and serves as a testament to their dedication and the foundation we collectively laid during our training sessions.

Over time, I've had the privilege of mentoring a diverse range of individuals, and it's consistently fulfilling to witness those who endure in the industry. It's particularly gratifying when individuals not only sustain their involvement but also display respect and gratitude for the guidance and support I've provided. While a few may never fully acknowledge my contributions, I'm at peace with that, and they themselves are aware of who they are.

More recently, in 2023, Hernandez and I embarked on a new endeavor by taking on the role of instructors. This initiative has allowed us to work directly with a fresh group of aspiring students. Engaging in both the training and creative processes with these upcoming wrestlers continues to be incredibly rewarding. The process of nurturing their talents and witnessing their growth as they embrace the rigorous demands of this profession is truly fulfilling.

The aspiration of establishing a thriving wrestling school has long been a personal goal of mine. Presently, it appears that, in collaboration with Shawn, we are indeed realizing this ambition. The journey, however, has been a deliberate and measured one. Guiding individuals within this industry demands patience, as it's not always easy to introduce new techniques to those with prior experience—after all, as the adage goes, teaching old dogs new tricks can be a challenge. Similarly, leading individuals to embrace new knowledge can sometimes prove challenging, similar to the saying "you can't always lead a horse to water."

Nonetheless, when that pivotal moment arrives and everything clicks for them, observing their remarkable progress is an indescribable sensation. Much of my inspiration as a trainer stems from Rudy Boy, himself an esteemed figure in this field. I've closely observed his evolution over the years and his adeptness in instructing aspiring wrestlers. Drawing from the lessons he imparted when I was just starting out is something I hold in high regard and consistently apply in my own teaching approach.

Having pursued a college education with the intention of becoming a teacher, I find myself naturally inclined towards an instructional role. Much of my teaching methodology is rooted in the valuable lessons I've learned from the mistakes I've made throughout my wrestling journey. While there are numerous decisions I would alter if given the chance, it's essential to emphasize that I carry no regrets for any aspect of my past. These experiences, even the ones I might change in hindsight, have collectively shaped the person I am within the dynamic realm of wrestling.

I alluded earlier in this text to the fact that I've had the privilege of participating in many of my students' and proteges' initial matches. This accomplishment brings an incomparable sense of achievement, as it entails turning someone's aspirations into reality. To be able to contribute to the fulfillment of their dreams is an immense honor and, truthfully, is a driving factor behind my commitment to what I do.

Collaborating with Shawn, I had the remarkable chance to create something truly distinctive: a kids' summer camp held during the months of June and July in 2023. You know, when you usually think of professional wrestling, it's often about tough, seasoned adults grappling in the ring. However, we got the chance to flip that script a bit.

At the Wrestling Shop in Rolling Oaks Mall in San Antonio Texas, we launched a two-month summer program tailored for kids aged 8 to 15. It was all about introducing them to the basic aspects of pro wrestling. And you know what? It turned out to be a whole lot of fun and really quite refreshing. Contrary to the usual image of wrestling, this venture allowed us to connect with a younger audience and give them a taste of what this sport is all about. Seeing their excitement and their eagerness to learn was truly heartwarming. This experience added a new layer to our involvement in wrestling, showing just how impactful this sport can be for people of all ages.

A big part of our interaction with these kids was making sure they understood how crucial safety is in this sport. We really wanted them to feel completely safe and to know that trying these moves at home is a no-go. What made it even more interesting was that the parents were there too, so we were educating not just the kids but also the parents about the ins and outs of this business.

Summer camp was a blast!

The safety of every single child in the camp was our absolute top priority. We took this commitment seriously. We made sure that every parent or guardian was right there at ringside, which not only underlined the importance of accountability but also allowed us to address any concerns immediately.

Plus, we were all about encouraging questions. Parents and students could ask us about specific moves, and we welcomed it. This approach really showed our dedication to creating a safe and educational environment for everyone involved.

What truly stands out about this camp is witnessing the organic development of characters right from the children themselves. One memorable individual among them was Kyle Clash, a kid who radiated charisma like no other, and even had a surplus of it. It's remarkable to note that some independent wrestlers I've encountered exhibit less charisma than what this kid possesses in his little pinky toe.

What adds to the charm of the whole experience is that many of these kids continue to attend events and watch the shows. It's both thrilling and intriguing to contemplate whether they will decide to pursue wrestling as grown men. In total, we had around nine kids, each bringing their own unique energy: Kyle Clash, Cade, Zack Attack, Phoenix Fire, Demon Fire, Zoko, J.E.G, The Maverick and Munchie.

The passion and talent these youngsters showcased were nothing short of incredible.

This whole journey has been immensely rewarding, providing a stark contrast to the drama and complications often associated with adult training and independent wrestling scenes. The prospect of what any of these young men might achieve in the future has me genuinely excited. Their potential seems boundless, and it's truly heartening to have been a part of nurturing it.

Looking back on the memories that really stand out, when it comes to mentoring and training in the wrestling world, I feel a strong sense of satisfaction. Being part of shaping the next generation in wrestling is something that means a lot to me—a responsibility that makes me proud but also keeps me grounded. Through mentoring, I've learned how to balance passing on technical skills with teaching values like safety, respect, and a strong commitment to this craft.

Remembering these instances, whether it was running a kids' summer camp or teaming up with Shawn to share the knowledge we've gained over the years, a diverse picture comes to mind. Seeing the excitement in the faces of these young enthusiasts, and even their parents, as they dive into the wrestling world, really drives home the thrill of this sport. Wrestling isn't just about what goes on in the ring; it's a mix of passion, friendship, and learning.

Moving beyond these experiences, it's worth noting the pro wrestlers I've had the privilege to mentor over time. Watching them grow from eager beginners to confident professionals has been incredibly satisfying. Seeing them develop unique personas and refine their skills to shine in the ring shows how mentorship and hard work can make a real impact. These individuals, just like the up-and-coming talents, have the potential to leave their mark on the wrestling scene.

All in all, this journey of mentoring highlights the mix of tradition and innovation, experience and enthusiasm, and the established generation and the newcomers. Wrestling's spirit goes beyond generations, and seeing these emerging talents find their place reminds me why I love this sport. It's a reminder that the passion for wrestling and its enduring essence keep growing, ensuring an exciting future that respects its history while looking ahead to new possibilities.

Passing down knowledge and experiences in wrestling is like keeping a flame alive. Just as I've learned from those who came before me, it's crucial for me to share what I've gained with the new generation of wrestlers. Wrestling isn't just about moves and matches; it's a heritage built on tradition and respect. The lessons I've learned over the years aren't just for me—they're meant to guide others too. Just as my mentors helped me, I want to provide guidance to those starting their journey.

The insights I've gathered go beyond the ring ropes. They encompass the psychology of wrestling, the importance of respect for opponents, and the value of connecting with the fans. These lessons are part of wrestling's fabric, passed on through stories and experiences. My mentors invested in me, and I want to invest in the next generation. Wrestling has its ups and downs, and I know how valuable a supportive guide can be. By sharing my knowledge, I'm not just aiding individual success; I'm carrying forward wrestling's essence.

Chapter 15
Behind the Curtain: From the Ring to the Booker's Chair

In a new chapter of my wrestling journey, May 2021 brought me a unique opportunity: the chance to step into the role of a booker for Austin Wrestling Revolution (AWR). This marked the first time I had been officially positioned in an office capacity. While in the past, I had often been regarded as a right-hand man, loosely involved in various capacities, including being a "match agent" for other promotions, this was my inaugural venture into directly shaping and orchestrating wrestling events. To be candid, I felt a bit out of my comfort zone and experienced moments of nervousness, especially as I engaged in tasks like reaching out to talent for show participation and helping determine match outcomes. Nonetheless, this was a long-held aspiration of mine, and I was eager to embrace the challenge.

AWR, which was established in 2017, provided the backdrop for this pivotal opportunity. My association with the company spanned several years, during which I had already been actively wrestling for them. It's worth noting that during this period, I held the esteemed title of heavyweight champion within the promotion, adding a layer of familiarity and rapport to my relationship with AWR.

Stepping into the role of a booker was a significant shift for me, transitioning from just a talent to a central player in shaping the shows' dynamics. The experience proved to be a blend of excitement and trepidation. As I worked through the intricacies of contacting talents and collaborating on match outcomes, I recognized the immense responsibility that came with the role. Yet, despite the initial challenges and uncertainties, it was an exhilarating experience that allowed me to contribute directly to the show's creative direction and overall success.

This new position marked a turning point in my wrestling journey, expanding my skill set and providing a deeper understanding of the intricacies of event coordination. Through this experience, I gained not only a greater appreciation for the multifaceted nature of wrestling promotions but also a renewed sense of drive to continue growing within this ever-evolving industry.

Me and Frito as AWR Tag Champions.

Rosario, also known in the wrestling world as Frito, initially took on the role of promoter for the promotion. Back when he laid the foundation for this venture, he sought out guidance and advice, and that's when he turned to me and Hernandez. We readily extended our support and mentorship, taking him under our wing. It's quite remarkable how he has since evolved into not only a proficient promoter but also a skilled heel worker. But, let's keep that just between us for now.

As we ventured into 2021, AWR was gradually making its presence felt in the local wrestling scene. The momentum was building, and we found ourselves securing shows at well-attended venues. In fact, we had ramped up to hosting two to three shows every month. In my initial month of booking responsibilities alone, I found myself juggling three shows right off the bat. It was an exciting time, but I'd be remiss if I didn't admit that there were moments of nerves.

Reaching out to the talent, discussing show dates, and coordinating their availability were aspects that initially gave me some jitters. It was a whole new level of interaction and responsibility for me. I needed to ensure everything was in place, attending to any concerns or requirements they might have. Those first steps into the role of booking exposed me to the behind-the-scenes intricacies of wrestling promotions, and it wasn't without its challenges.

But as time progressed, those initial butterflies transformed into a rhythm. The camaraderie we had built with the talent made conversations flow more smoothly. It's a unique experience, getting to know the wrestlers on a professional level while making sure everything aligns seamlessly for the shows. Looking back, those initial apprehensions feel like a distant memory compared to the confidence and knowledge I've gained through the experience.

I've really grown into this role, and I've learned pretty fast that it's all about rolling with the punches. You can plan and book shows way in advance, but when the actual show day arrives, you're faced with a whirlwind of variables. Cars might conk out, people might change their minds about showing up, some might disappear into thin air, and then there's the whole thing of managing the egos and moods of talents who suddenly decide they're out for whatever reason. You've got to keep moving forward, no matter what.

Another thing that's become clear is that, as a booker, you're often the one who gets the blame when things go wrong, even if it's not your fault. When others drop the ball or make unexpected calls, it usually falls on the booker's shoulders. But despite the challenges, this has been a serious learning experience. After being a wrestler for 21 years, seeing this side of the business and soaking up all these lessons has definitely opened my eyes.

What I've come to understand over these years is that wrestling is more than just the moves in the ring —it's like this intricate puzzle of logistics, personalities, and the art of steering the ship even in rough waters. It's like mastering the rhythm of a constantly shifting tide. This switch from being just a performer to becoming a booker has shown me parts of the wrestling world I had no clue about before. It's broadened my perspective, deepened my love for the craft, and given me insights that I know will shape my journey in ways I can't even imagine yet.

This new role I've taken on has truly enhanced my understanding of the wrestling business like never before. In addition to that, I've also been playing a bit of an ambassadorial role within the local wrestling community. I've been actively reaching out to other promotions, such as Dogg Pound Championship Wrestling, which is spearheaded by Jazz and Rodney Mack—two individuals who have a solid foundation in old school wrestling and its traditions. They've graciously welcomed us with open arms on multiple occasions, and getting to know them has been an incredible experience.

Working with the great talent they have raised up has been amazing, guys like Midnight Special, Hoss Holding, Caramel Lightning, Mystii Marks and Nate Greysin has been a pleasure.

With Jazz & Rodney Mack

Beyond that, I've had the chance to reconnect with familiar faces from my past, such as those at PWI getting back in touch with old friends like Marcello Franco and Roland . The objective is all about creating alliances and fostering collaborations. It's about exchanging talent and joining forces to cultivate a more positive environment within the local scene. This endeavor is about more than just individual promotions; it's about collectively enhancing the wrestling landscape.

Being part of these interactions has been both enlightening and heartening. It's a reminder that despite the competitiveness, there's a shared appreciation for the sport and a genuine desire to elevate it collectively. These connections have underscored the importance of unity within the wrestling community. It's about moving beyond rivalries and working together to bring out the best in both performers and promotions, fostering an environment that thrives on mutual respect and growth.

For the longest time, the prevailing wisdom was that you should stick with one promotion and follow their rules exclusively. But what I've come to understand is that a more effective approach for the indy wrestling scene is all about working together. This mindset even extends to the national level—we've seen how AEW, Ring of Honor, TNA, and Japanese promotions collaborate to co-promote events. If a local promotion insists that the local fan base should only support them, it can create unnecessary competition for the same audience. However, the reality is that there's a great potential for everyone to team up and create entertaining shows that benefit all.

Forming connections with other promotions has been incredibly rewarding. Building working relationships with different companies and directly engaging with fellow promoters and bookers has brought about numerous benefits. It not only expands opportunities for wrestlers and fans but also demonstrates the power of unity within the wrestling community.

It's really heartening to see how collaboration can lead to mutual success. By sharing resources, talents, and ideas, the potential for putting on remarkable shows skyrockets. Wrestling has such a diverse landscape, and when different promotions combine their strengths, the result can be an exceptional experience for everyone involved.

In essence, shifting away from the idea of rigid loyalty to a single promotion has opened up a world of possibilities. This change in perspective has illuminated the path to building connections and forming meaningful partnerships that ultimately contribute to the greater success of not just individual promotions, but the entire indy wrestling realm.

A core element of AWR's identity is rooted in an old-school mindset, particularly when it comes to showmanship. Our goal is to stand out from the crowd. Instead of relying solely on flashy high spots and purposeless aerial stunts, our focus is on nurturing talent that can embody larger-than-life characters reminiscent of the '80s and '90s. Athletic prowess isn't the sole criterion; our mission is to help every wrestler reach their full potential.

We place a strong emphasis on fostering individuals who not only embrace learning but also radiate positive attitudes. Our aim is to bring back the true essence of wrestling as an art form—one that encompasses more than just physical skills. It's about charisma, storytelling, and forging a genuine connection with the audience. This approach has earned AWR a well-deserved reputation as a hidden gem in the state's wrestling scene. Despite minimal investment in marketing, our shows consistently captivate and entertain.

Over time, AWR has transitioned from a fledgling promotion to a thriving entity that I'm profoundly proud to be a part of. Much of this transformation can be credited to Hernandez's creative brilliance and Frito's steadfast commitment, along with my own dedicated efforts. Together, we're on a mission to create something truly remarkable.

This journey hasn't been without its challenges, and it involves a significant amount of hard work. Yet, our passion for what we're building fuels our determination. We're committed to recapturing the essence of wrestling that enthralled fans for generations. Every step we take, every show we put together, is a testament to our unwavering dedication to preserving that spirit. As we continue to grow, our aim is to leave a lasting mark known for quality, dedication, and a profound love for the art of wrestling.

I love being a part of AWR!

AWR stands out to me as the most incredible environment and locker room I've had the privilege to be a part of during my extensive 20-plus years in wrestling. What makes it even more special is the fact that I have a direct role in shaping its future. Since those early days, our journey has been nothing short of remarkable, marked by countless shows that have sometimes reached the impressive number of 20 to 25 per year.

One of the standout moments in this journey was the opportunity to organize events on the grounds of Fort Sam Houston, performing in front of our dedicated troops. The distinct honor of entertaining those who serve our country is a memory etched deeply in my heart. Moreover, our relationships with local venues and bars have contributed to our growth and outreach, broadening our connection with the community.

What's truly astounding is the steady influx of exceptionally talented individuals who have graced our promotion. Our doors have witnessed a constant stream of gifted wrestlers, each bringing their unique flavor to our shows. Admittedly, it hasn't been a smooth ride, and we've faced our share of challenges. Yet, through perseverance and dedication, things have fallen into place in ways I could have never envisioned. Being on this side of the wrestling business has granted me insights and satisfaction beyond my wildest expectations.

It's worth acknowledging the pivotal roles played by Frito and Hernandez in entrusting me with the position of booker. Their faith in my abilities has been pivotal in shaping AWR's trajectory. This new avenue of business was uncharted territory for me, and the experience has been nothing short of amazing. As I delved deeper into this aspect of wrestling, I found myself growing and evolving in ways I hadn't anticipated.

AWR has become more than just a wrestling promotion to me—it's a canvas of growth, collaboration, and evolution. Our journey has been marked by challenges, triumphs, and the unwavering passion that drives us to deliver memorable shows. Looking ahead, I'm excited about the endless possibilities that lie before us. The shared dedication of the team, the resilience in the face of adversity, and the constant quest to enhance the wrestling experience all converge to create a future that's nothing short of promising.

My involvement with AWR has also contributed significantly to my personal growth and maturity. Back when I was just one of the guys, I used to be all about the ribbing and light-hearted teasing, often going overboard. I relished in busting people's chops and being a prankster. However, since taking on a more official role, that dynamic has shifted. As part of what you could call the "office," my demeanor has transformed into one that's calm, composed, and collected. This shift has become particularly evident when shows don't quite go as planned, and I'm tasked with maintaining a level head despite the chaos.

Interestingly, this transition has also bolstered my confidence in engaging with a wide array of individuals. Previously, I would have never pictured myself orchestrating discussions with potential show venues or initiating meetings to delve into the business side of professional wrestling. In the past, my perspective was somewhat naive, centered around my identity solely as a professional wrestler. Now, with my responsibilities extended beyond the ring, I've been exposed to a whole new dimension of the wrestling world. It was admittedly daunting at first, as I dived headfirst into uncharted territory when the keys to this new role were handed to me.

This journey has forced me to evolve not only as a wrestling professional but also as a person. It's about adapting my approach, understanding the nuances of negotiation, and learning to navigate unanticipated hurdles with composure. This new chapter has demanded a level of maturity and awareness that goes beyond the comradery I was used to. Striking that balance between being the guy who brings the fun and the guy who keeps the ship steady has been an incredible learning curve—one that's been as rewarding as it's been challenging.

Essentially, this evolution embodies the broader theme of AWR itself—growth, adaptation, and embracing the unexpected. As the pages of this chapter continue to unfold, I'm excited to see how this transformation will continue to shape both my journey and the wrestling world around me. From a young, enthusiastic wrestler to someone who navigates the multifaceted aspects of promotion, this journey has undoubtedly enriched my understanding of wrestling and my place within it.

Chapter 16
From the Mat to the Heart: Closing Reflections

This book's journey spans over two decades, and it's quite amusing to admit that I was actually getting into its initial draft while I was knee-deep in training for pro wrestling back in 2001. A bit embarrassingly, I was literally writing it while I was wrestling. My intention was to capture the essence of those moments in real time, just like Mick Foley did with his first book —pen to paper and then onto the screen. Funny enough, that early draft of the book ballooned to four times the size of what you're holding now. I remember sitting in my government class during my junior year, jotting down my thoughts instead of focusing on the subject matter at hand.

And now, here I am, typing away on my computer screen, feeling a wave of nostalgia and reflection. It's incredible to see how far I've come, how much I've learned, all thanks to wrestling's steady presence in my life. Looking back, it's hard to fathom where I'd be today if I hadn't ventured into professional wrestling. The trajectory of my life would have been dramatically different.

Looking back, it's kind of wild to imagine how different things could have turned out if I hadn't jumped into the world of professional wrestling. I mean, seriously, I would've missed out on meeting so many amazing people who've become lifelong friends. These are connections that came out of the wrestling scene and have added some serious depth to my life.

Wrestling isn't all glitz and glam; it's had its share of challenges. Those conflicts and setbacks I've faced in this world have been like crash courses in building up my resilience. It's like each hurdle was a chance to toughen up and grow stronger. It definitely wasn't easy, but it's made me who I am today.

This whole wrestling journey has been a roller coaster of emotions, too. I got to experience that heart-pounding rush of falling in love for the first time right in the midst of all the wrestling action. And then, of course, came the heartbreak that hit like a freight train. Those emotions, raw and real, have given me a new perspective on relationships.

But wrestling isn't just about the physical stuff; it's taught me some pretty serious life lessons. I've learned about what it means to be a man through the ups and downs of this crazy journey. And trust me, I've had some close calls in the ring that reminded me just how precious life is.

This was a dream come true for me as a teen.

Thinking back to where it all began, it's kind of nuts that it started as a simple teenage dream. Sitting in school, sneaking glances at local wrestling shows, and daydreaming about stepping into that ring as a pro wrestler—it all seemed so far-fetched. But here I am now, looking at how this dream has turned into a whole life path that's molded me in ways I never saw coming.

I didn't write this book to claim I've hit some huge stardom level or become a mega-success in the wrestling world. I've never scored a national contract that plastered my face all over billboards. But that doesn't mean I haven't racked up enough stories and experiences to make sharing them worthwhile. And if you've stuck around to read this far, I've got to say a big thank you. Your interest in my journey means the world to me.

Sure, what I've shared here might feel like just a scratch on the surface. There are countless tales still itching to be told, and who knows, maybe a second book will give them the spotlight they deserve. This is just a sneak peek, a brief dive into the tumultuous world of wrestling and my little part in it all.

As time marches on, I still feel that fire burning within me. There's a whole lot more to uncover and explore. Lately, I've been toying with the idea of stepping away from the ring and into a behind-the-scenes role—management, refereeing, who knows? Regardless of where I end up, one thing remains constant: my connection to this business. It's like an unbreakable thread that's woven itself into my life.

Throughout my journey, I've faced my fair share of challenges. People have tried to sideline me, naysayers have attempted to put me out of the game, and voices have whispered that I don't belong. But here's the thing: I've never let that sway me. No matter what, I've held tight to who I am. The wrestling world might be chaotic, but I've found my own groove, evolving while staying true to myself. It's been a ride, and it's far from over.

Over the years, I've collected a bunch of experiences that are etched in my memory. These moments, big and small, have stuck with me. And in this journey, the wrestling world has dished out lessons that are like golden rules. One of the biggest takeaways? Never throw in the towel. I know, it sounds like a cheesy line from a movie, but if you're eyeing a career in wrestling, it's more than just words—it's a mindset to live by.

As I've navigated this world, one thing has become clear: your attitude shapes your wrestling journey. If you walk into the arena in a bad mood, things might not go so well. I've seen loads of folks stumble not because they lacked skill, but because they couldn't accept their own limits. Attitude, my friend, is a game-changer. When I'm mentoring and training newcomers, I can often tell from their attitude if they've got what it takes, even if it's just on the local scene. And remember, it's not about how far you go; it's about having the guts to try, even if you stumble along the way.

Every time I go out to perform I love it!

I've had plenty of talks with folks who want to step into the wrestling world but hesitate because of age or size concerns. Here's the scoop: wrestling isn't one-size-fits-all. It embraces all kinds of talents, shapes, and sizes. And guess what? I've talked to so many who held back due to self-doubt. I've also heard stories of those who jumped in but realized it wasn't their thing. The wrestling path is full of twists, but here's the deal: Don't talk about it, be about it.

So, here's the deal: don't underestimate yourself. Don't let anyone else define your limits. Wrestling and life have a lot in common—there are unexpected turns, but your attitude and determination can steer the ship. To all you dreamers reading this, especially those who dream of wrestling, remember this: drown out the negativity, chase those dreams, and let your journey unfold as it should. Your dreams are worth every effort you put in.

Sometimes, it's important for our dreams to be grounded in reality. And while I don't want to come off as bragging or embellishing my achievements, there are certain facts that stand strong. I managed to achieve what I set out to do in this business—have my first match. Over a span of more than two decades, I've been a part of the wrestling world, grappling with legends whose names echo through the industry. Looking back, I've demonstrated the kind of tenacity and spirit that outshines a good number of those who've come and gone.

Now, let's be clear—I'm no stranger to making mistakes. Life and this business have both been arenas where I've tripped up. Yet, that's exactly why I wanted to pen down this book—to share how I navigated those stumbles and held onto my principles. I'm not here to boast; I'm here to show you that perseverance can be a guiding star, even in a world as unpredictable as wrestling.

So, for those of you who are truly set on becoming a wrestler, even if it's just on a local level, let me say this: go for it. No one can deny the reality of what you accomplish in this business. Sure, our dreams need a dose of realism, but remember that every step you take towards your goal, no matter how small, is a stride towards living your passion. And while mistakes and setbacks might dot your path, they're just a part of the journey. Embrace them, learn from them, and let your spirit be your driving force.

There's something I want to dive into here. Over the last few years, I've been making an effort to tie up loose ends. Through my journey, I've had to chew on some pride and own up to some mistakes. There were instances where I might have inadvertently rubbed people the wrong way, or maybe even knowingly. It's become clear to me that sometimes the best approach is to put that pride aside, speak my truth, and then decide whether to agree to disagree or join forces.

I've come to understand that life is too fleeting for grudges to take center stage. Wrestling, no matter how intense, shouldn't overshadow the potential for lasting friendships or meaningful relationships. It's a lesson that's often easier said than done, but it's one that's worth embracing. As I've journeyed through this business, I've come to appreciate the value of reconciliation and collaboration. It's a reminder that growth isn't just about honing moves in the ring, but about evolving as a person, owning up to past actions, and making amends when necessary.

In my early career, I made a big mistake by leaving ACW on bad terms in 2002, creating lingering discord. But this laid the groundwork for a real-life lesson five years later. I unexpectedly showed up at an ACW show, having gained more wisdom as a wrestler. This reunion was my chance to mend things with

Prince Fontenot and prove my growth since the 2001 misstep. We talked it out, delving into our shared history openly.

No ego or pride, I owned up to letting emotions guide me wrong and flat-out apologized for the drama that soured our connection in 2001. Importantly, I respected his ACW achievements, showing how I'd evolved since our clashes. Surprisingly, he felt the same, recognizing where we went wrong on both sides. Time had healed, moving us beyond old grudges.

Relief flooded in. Tension dissolved, giving way to freedom and a fresh start. Setting aside differences felt liberating. This underscored the power of forgiveness and owning mistakes. I thanked him for his ACW support in 2001 and grasped his perspective. Our reconciliation marked a key moment, emphasizing humility and growth in an evolving industry.

Everything I've done or said in this business has come from a place of good intentions and has been shaped by my own mistakes. If you're reading this and there's something left unresolved between us, I want you to know that you can always reach out and talk to me. I've grown a lot during my time in this business, and I believe many others I've been associated with have also evolved as the years have gone by. And believe me, over two decades in this business is a pretty long stretch.

Life's a journey of change, and the wrestling world isn't immune to it either. If there's something between us that's lingering, don't let it hold you back. We've all matured and shifted our perspectives as we've navigated through this ever-changing field. The wrestling landscape itself has gone through its own series of transformations, reflecting the growth we've all undergone.

So, if you're looking back and thinking about unfinished conversations, just know that it's never too late to bridge the gap. We've all been shaped by this business in one way or another, and part of that growth is recognizing the importance of resolving things that are left hanging. Life's too short to carry grudges, and in a world that's seen over two decades of shifts, it's clear that change is the only constant.

As I've mentioned earlier, the wrestling scene has seen its fair share of ups and downs. But through it all, one thing remains unchanged: who I am at my core. I'm still that Eric Perez who used to roam the halls of Judson High School, dreaming of making it into the ring. I remember those days of hustling to get a spot in ACW matches at the Texas Hideaway flea market, and eventually working my way up to being part of Rudy Boy Gonzales' Texas Wrestling Academy.

This journey has taken me across the state, from one wrestling event to the next. I've covered countless miles, shared the road with fellow wrestlers on memorable trips, and faced off against some incredible opponents in unforgettable matches. These moments have become the vibrant memories that define my wrestling career. And you know what? I wouldn't trade any of it for the world.

When I look back, I can honestly say I have no regrets. Every victory, every setback—they've all played a role in shaping who I am today. From the eager teenager at Judson High School to the seasoned wrestler standing here now, each phase has left its mark. And if I had the chance to change anything, I'd still choose the same path.

So, as I reflect on this journey, I'm filled with a sense of fulfillment. The road I've traveled, the friendships I've built, the lessons I've learned—they're all part of my wrestling story. It's a journey that's defined me, one that's led me through some of the most significant moments of my life. Looking back, I can confidently say that every step was worth it.

My first promo pic in 2001.

Special Thanks

First and foremost, I want to thank God, my parents, and my family. Back when I was just a 16-year-old, I was a mix of nervous and excited diving into my dream. Looking back, I can't believe how lucky I've been to get so many chances to step into that ring and perform for all of you.

To all the fans who ever bought a ticket to watch me wrestle, I seriously can't thank you enough. Your support is what keeps me going. And even though I never hit the big leagues, I'm grateful for every single moment I've spent wrestling.

Big shout out to all the mentors, trainers, old-timers, and promoters who've been there every step of the way. Your advice and backing mean everything. And to all the wrestlers young and old I've had the chance to work with and share my knowledge with, thanks for letting me give back to the sport I love.

There's way too many to name but you know who you are. Thank you for trusting me with your health and safety in the ring and thank you for taking care of me as well. Thank you to Shawn and Rosario, the other two heads of the "three headed monster". Thanks to Carey Martell for proofreading this book.

To my buddies and colleagues who've been on this journey with me, I'll always cherish the memories we've made together. And to my family, you've had my back through thick and thin – thank you for being my rock.

As I think about the past 20 plus years, I'm just really thankful for every moment. Thanks to each and every one of you for being part of this wild ride. Your support and love have kept me going, and I truly believe the best is still ahead.

THE BEST IS YET TO COME.

Printed in Great Britain
by Amazon